CAROL VORDERMAN
English Made Easy

10
Minutes
A Day
Spelling

Ages
7–11

DK

Consultant Claire White

This timer counts up to 10 minutes.
When it reaches 10:00, it will beep.

How to use the timer:

Switch the timer ON.
Press the triangle ▶ to START the timer.
Press the square ■ to STOP or PAUSE the timer.
Press the square ■ to RESET the timer to 00:00.
Press any button to WAKE UP the timer.

 Penguin
Random
House

Senior Editor Deborah Lock
Editor Rohini Deb
English Consultant Claire White
Art Editor Jyotsna Khosla
Design Consultant Shefali Upadhyay
Deputy Managing Editor Soma B. Chowdhury
Managing Art Editor Richard Czapnik
Art Director Martin Wilson
DTP Designer Sachin Gupta
Production Editor Francesca Wardell

First published in Great Britain by
Dorling Kindersley Limited
80 Strand, London, WC2R 0RL

Copyright © 2014 Dorling Kindersley Limited
A Penguin Company
11 10 9 8 7
010–197388–Jan/2014

A CIP catalogue record for this book
is available from the British Library
ISBN: 978-1-4093-4143-7

Printed and bound in China

All images © Dorling Kindersley Limited
For further information see: www.dkimages.com

A WORLD OF IDEAS:
SEE ALL THERE IS TO KNOW

www.dk.com

Contents

Time taken

Time filler:
In these boxes are some extra challenges to extend your skills. You can do them if you have some time left after finishing the questions and continue until you hear the 10-minute beep. Or, these can be stand-alone activities that you can do in 10 minutes.

Syllables and stresses

To make spelling words less tricky, split them into syllables.
Press the timer and let us get started!

(1) Count the syllables in these words.

supermarket [4]   gardening [3]   furious [3]

adventure [3]   preparation [4]   journey [2]

(2) Link together the words that have the same number of syllables.

colour   dangerous   picture   afterwards

family   shadow   introduce   outside

(3) Look at the pictures of these two-syllable words. The second syllable has been given. Have a go at spelling the first syllable.

tre**sure**

pres**ent**

(4) Look at the pictures of these two-syllable words. The first syllable has been given. Have a go at spelling the second syllable.

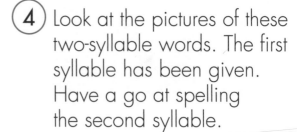

wiz**erd**

whis**tle**

5 A part of each label is given. Look at each picture and complete its label. How many syllables does each word have?

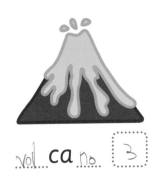 vol ca no 3

 water fall 2

 moun tain 2

6 When one syllable is longer and louder, it is a **stressed** syllable. Circle words that are stressed at the beginning, and cross out those at the end.

~~demand~~   ~~restore~~   ~~forget~~   (table)   (famous)

7 These words are spelt the same, but have different meanings when the stress changes. For each word, put a tick mark in the noun or verb column.

Word	Noun	Verb
record	✓	
re**cord**		✓
progress	✓	
pro**gress**		✓

Are the nouns stressed at the beginning or at the end?   beginning

8 Write your name and circle the stress. How many syllables are there?

(Aa)ron 2   (Ma)ini 2

Origins of prefixes

A prefix is added to the beginning of a root word. It changes the meaning of the word. Try them out!

1 Complete this chart of prefixes that have come from the Latin language. For each prefix, use a dictionary to write two more words, and then work out their meanings.

Prefix	Example 1	Example 2	Example 3	Meaning of prefix
aqu-	aqueduct	aqua	aquas	water
pro-	proceed	produce	poject	forward
im-	import	immature	impossible	not
in-, ir-, il-	incorrect			
pre-	preview			
re-	redo			
sub-	submarine			
super-	superstar			
ex-	external			
co-	co-writer			
de-	defrost			

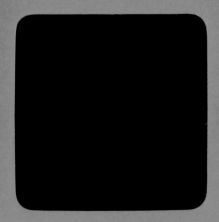

Time filler:
How many words, with three or more letters, can you make with the letters in "investigation"? Here are three words to get you started: "vote", "gain" and "sting".

2 Complete this chart of prefixes that have come from the Greek language. For each prefix, use a dictionary to write two more words, and then work out their meanings.

Prefix	Example 1	Example 2	Example 3	Meaning of prefix
anti-	anticlockwise			
auto-	autograph			
kilo-	kilogram			
cy-	cyclone			
dyna-	dynasty			
geo-	geography			
micro-	microscope			
mis-	misbehave			
peri-	periscope			
mono-	monorail			
bio-	biology			

Root words

Root words are the forms of words without any prefixes or suffixes added. How well can you recognise them?

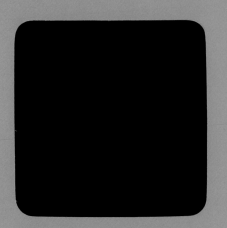

1) Complete this chart of Latin and Greek root words. For each root word, use a dictionary to write two more words based on this root word, and then work out its meaning.

Root word	Example 1	Example 2	Example 3	Meaning of root word
dict	dictate			
pel	repel			
scrib	describe			
gress	progress			
tract	attract			
vert	divert			
ject	eject			
dem	democracy			
chron	synchronise			
path	sympathy			
phon	telephone			
gram/graph	diagram			
therm	hypothermia			
scope	telescope			

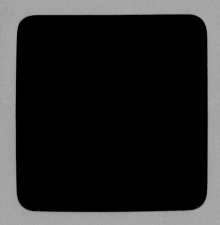

Time filler:
A useful way to learn spellings is to find complete words within words. For example, remember the spelling of "thousand" by finding the word "sand" within it. Now try to find complete words within these words: "fortunate", "emigrate", "apparent" and "correspond".

② The following words are French in origin:
words with "sh" sound spelt **ch**, such as "chef";
words with "g" sound spelt **gue**, such as "tongue";
words with "k" sound spelt **que**, such as "unique".

Words with "s" sound spelt **sc**, such as "science", are Latin in origin.
Words with "k" sound spelt **ch**, such as "chorus", are Greek in origin.

Say each of the following words aloud, and then write them under the French, Italian (Latin) or Greek flags to identify the origin of the words.

school	scene	chalet	antique
chauffeur	chemist	fascinate	scissors
league	anchor	muscle	character

French

Italian (Latin)

Greek

Spelling suffixes

A suffix is a group of letters placed at the end of a word to make a new word. Some suffixes change the meaning of the word.
Let's try some of these.

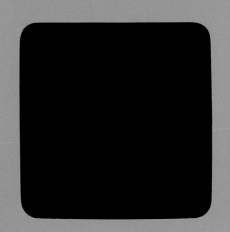

1 Complete this chart of common suffixes. For each suffix, use a dictionary to write two more words based on this suffix, and then work out their meanings.

Suffix	Example 1	Example 2	Example 3	Meaning of suffix
-ship	membership			
-hood	childhood			
-ness	kindness			
-ment	enjoyment			
-less	helpless			
-dom	kingdom			
-some	wholesome			
-craft	handicraft			
-ology	biology			
-ward	downward			
-ism	criticism			

Time filler:
Another useful way to know the spelling of tricky words is to learn a phrase that uses the letters in order. For example, for the word "geography", remember: Greg Egg's Old Grandmother Rode a Pig Home Yesterday. Make your own phrases for words that you find tricky to spell.

2) Make words by combining each word with one of the suffixes: **-ness**, **-ment** or **-ship**. Remember: If the word ends in a consonant and a **y**, change the **y** to an **i** before adding the suffix.

silly ....   agree ....   drowsy ....

merry ....   partner ....   close ....

3) More than one suffix can sometimes be added. Write these words.

fear + some + ness = ...

care + less + ness = ...

4) Complete the words in the chart with the vowel suffixes **-ive**, **-ic** or **-ist**.

Suffix **-ive**	Suffix **-ic**	Suffix **-ist**
respons..........	horrif..........	violin..........
act..........	terrif..........	special..........
decorat..........	histor..........	art..........
narrat..........	allerg..........	journal..........

What happens to the root words ending in **e**? ....

What happens to the root words ending in **y**? ....

"le" sound

There are a number of spelling patterns that make the "le" sound. These are mostly a combination of two letters (digraphs): a vowel and the consonant **l**.

1 The most common spelling of the "le" sound at the end of a root word is **le**. Join the rhyming words.

| settle | wiggle | tumble | buckle |

| rumble | dimple | kettle | saddle |

| simple | chuckle | paddle | giggle |

2 Other spelling patterns that may be used for the "le" sound are **el** or **al**. In a few words, **il** or **ol** is used. Complete these words. Use a dictionary if needed.

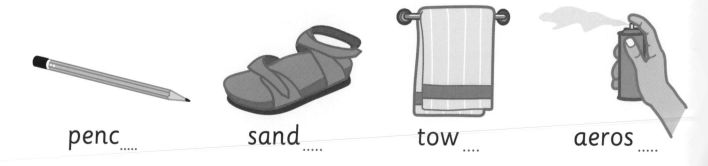

penc.....   sand.....   tow....   aeros.....

3 The "le" sound can be a suffix ending. The letters **al** are used when changing nouns to adjectives. **Note:** Sometimes the spelling of the noun must be changed slightly before adding **al**.

continent + al = ...   navy + al = ...

music + al = ...   nation + al = ...

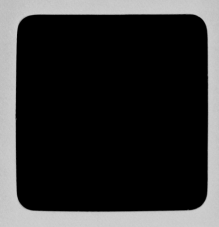

Time filler:
Create your own crossword with words that end in the "le" sound. Use a dictionary to help you write the clues. To begin with, use words such as "resemble", "horrible", "festival", "mineral", "miracle" and "punctual".

4 Complete the crossword. The first three letters of each word are given to you. All words have the "le" sound at the end. Use a dictionary to find the words.

Across
1. Having very hot and humid conditions (tro)
2. A celebration on the street (car)
3. A round shape (cir)
4. The remains of prehistoric living things (fos)
5. Furniture you eat at (tab)

Down
1. A human-made underground passage (tun)
2. An item or object (art)
3. A mystery or a game with interlocking pieces (puz)
4. A warm-blooded animal that has fur (mam)
5. A large building with thick walls, towers and battlements (cas)

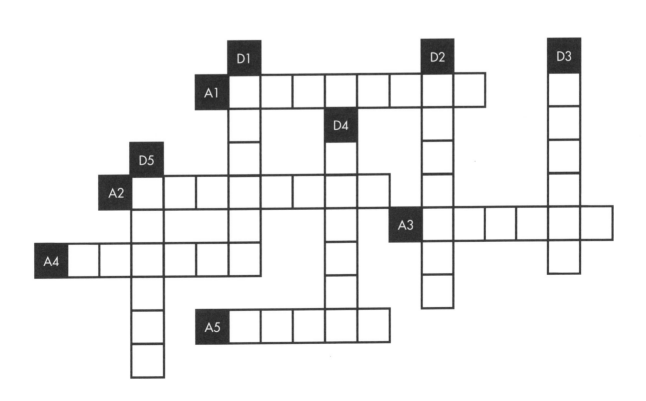

14

Comparing adjectives

Find out what happens to adjectives when you start comparing things.

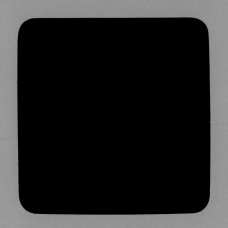

1 Add **er** to words when you compare two things (**comparative**) and **est** when something is of the highest order (**superlative**). Complete the sentences.

Max   Tom   Sam

Max is fast, Tom is _____ and Sam is the _____ .

Tim   Dad   Grandad

Tim is tall, Dad is _____ and Grandad is the _____ .

2 For words ending with an **e**, just add **r** or **st**. Complete the sentence.

Pine
Palm
Apple

The apple tree is large, the palm is_____, and the pine is the _____ .

3 For words ending with a vowel and a single consonant, double the consonant and add the ending. Complete the sentence.

Great Dane
Greyhound
Collie

The Collie is big, the Greyhound is _____, but the Great Dane is the _____

4 For words ending with a consonant and a **y**, change the **y** to **i** and add the ending. Use the word "angry" to complete the sentence.

John is angry, Jane is _____ and Justin is the _____ .

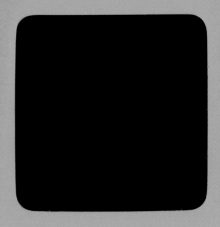

Time filler:
Write a funny poem comparing yourself with the other members of your family. Compare what you look like and what you do. Underline the comparative and superlative adjectives that you have used.

(5) For most three-syllable adjectives and some two-syllable adjectives, use "more" for the comparative and "most" for the superlative. Add "more" and "most" to this sentence.

The gardener is knowledgeable about plants. The tree surgeon is .... knowledgeable than the gardener. The botanist is the .... knowledgeable of all the plant lovers.

(6) Complete the chart with the comparatives and the superlatives.

Adjective	Comparative	Superlative
slow		
wet		
important		
happy		

(7) There are some irregular adjectives that do not follow these spelling rules. Can you link the adjective to its comparative and superlative?

Adjective	Comparative	Superlative
good	worse	best
bad	farther	least
little	better	worst
far	less	farthest

"Not" prefixes

The prefixes **in**-, **im**-, **ir**- and **il**- all mean "not". Also, **un**-, **dis**- and **de**- mean "not" and are used as exceptions. Try these out!

---

(1) The prefix **in**- is used most often. Write these words.

not direct = ...

not active = ...

not accurate = ...

not capable = ...

(2) Add **ir**- to root words beginning with **r**, making a double **r**. Write these words.

not regular = ...

not responsible = ...

not replaceable = ...

---

(3) Add **il**- to root words beginning with **l**, making a double **l**. Write these words.

not legal = ...

not legible = ...

not logical = ...

(4) Add **im**- to some root words beginning with **m** and **p**. Write these words.

not mobile = ...

not proper = ...

not possible = ...

---

(5) There are exceptions to the above rules. Circle the words spelt correctly.

defrost or infrost   irreasonable or unreasonable

illike or dislike   depart or inpart

unload or ilload   implease or displease

Time filler:
How many words, with three or more letters, can you make with the letters in "immediately"? Here are three words to get you started: "team", "lime" and "meal".

(6) Add a prefix to each of these root words in the word search.
Think about how the prefix changes the meaning of the root word.

credible   aware   polite   code   order

accurate   patient   made   compose   modest

i	n	c	r	e	d	i	b	l	e
m	r	i	a	i	e	u	t	n	v
p	e	m	p	r	c	n	i	i	u
a	d	p	r	o	o	m	s	m	n
t	r	o	l	m	d	a	d	m	a
i	o	l	d	t	e	d	s	o	w
e	s	i	e	o	p	e	i	d	a
n	i	t	s	d	i	s	d	e	r
t	d	e	c	o	m	p	o	s	e
i	n	a	c	c	u	r	a	t	e

Changing y

The "igh" or "ee" sound
at the end of a word is
often spelt with the letter **y**.
Listen out for them!

① Add the letter **y** to these words and use the words to complete the
sentences. **Hint:** For some short words, double the last consonant.

| crisp | fuss | sun | run | fur | full |

The bacon tasted ....

The day was hot and ....

The kitten was ....

The toddler was ....

The gravy was ....

The restaurant was .... booked.

② These words end with an **e**. Add the letter **y** to them.
Hint: Drop the **e** to add the **y**.

bone   smoke   stone   grease   laze

....

Why is the **e** removed? ....

....

③ Circle the words with **y** as an "igh" sound.
Cross out the words with **y** as an "ee" sound.

cry   boy   hurry   stay   happy   apply

What is different about the **y** in the words not circled or crossed out?

....

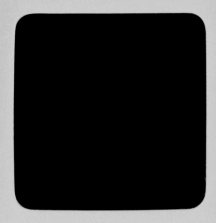

Time filler:
Here is a rhyme to help you remember the spelling of "difficulty": Mrs D, Mrs I, Mrs FFI, Mrs C, Mrs U, Mrs LTY. Try this method with the words "similarity" and "tremendous".

④ Find 10 words from page 18 in this word search.

h	a	b	m	r	h	o	t	b	y
u	n	o	n	l	a	z	y	m	g
r	u	n	n	y	p	a	l	p	r
r	o	y	u	a	p	p	l	y	e
y	m	g	l	p	y	d	n	f	a
b	f	u	l	s	a	f	n	o	s
p	u	f	z	y	l	u	s	s	y
z	s	m	o	k	y	l	a	g	l
l	s	f	r	m	f	l	r	r	t
o	y	t	g	s	s	y	t	f	m

Useful word list 1

Read each column of words.
Next, cover the words up one
by one and write them. Then
move on to the next column.

Monday	....	tonight	....
Tuesday	....	today	....
Wednesday	....	month	....
Thursday	....	morning	....
Friday	....	afternoon	....
Saturday	....	season	....
Sunday	....	winter	....
holiday	....	spring	....
yesterday	....	summer	....
tomorrow	....	autumn	....
birthday	....	January	....
anniversary	....	February	....
weekend	....	March	....
fortnight	....	April	....

Time filler:
Choose five words from this list and use each one in its own sentence. Keep coming back to these lists to check that you still know these useful words.

May	....	seventeen	....
June	....	eighteen	....
July	....	nineteen	....
August	....	twenty	....
September	....	thirty	....
October	....	forty	....
November	....	fifty	....
December	....	sixty	....
eleven	....	seventy	....
twelve	....	eighty	....
thirteen	....	ninety	....
fourteen	....	hundred	....
fifteen	....	thousand	....
sixteen	....	million	....

Tricky plurals

To make nouns plural,
you usually add **s**.
But for many words,
it is not as easy as that.

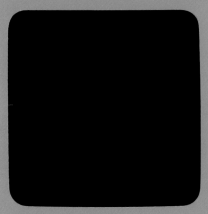

---

(1) Add **es** to each word with hissing endings: **s**, **x**, **z**, **sh**, **ch** or **ss**.

brush ....   glass ....   match ....

---

(2) For words ending in a consonant and a **y**, change **y** to **i** and add **es**.

puppy ....   pony ....   city ....

---

(3) Add **s** to most words ending in an **o**.

piano ....   solo ....   yo-yo ....

There are exceptions to this rule. Add **es** to make these words plural.

potato ....   volcano ....   cargo ....

---

(4) For words ending in an **ff**, just add **s**.

cuff ....   sniff ....   puff ....

---

(5) For words ending in an **f** or **fe**, change the **f** or **fe** to **v** and add **es**.

half ....   leaf ....   knife ....

There are exceptions to this rule. Just add **s** to make these words plural.

roof ....   chief ....

6 Some words change completely when made plural.
Match each word to its plural.

 child

geese

mouse

cacti

goose

children

cactus

mice

7 Some other words stay the same when made plural.
Circle these words below.

deer   monkey   sheep   fish   cat

8 Complete the sentences using the plural of these words.

half	fox	loaf	life	foot

Jan cut the pizza into two ....

In the field, a fox ran to join the other ....

The baker cooked ten .... of bread.

The proverb says a cat has nine ....

The girl hopped on one foot, then she jumped on two ....

Silent letters

Over 60% of English words have silent letters. Many of these letters were pronounced in the past. Some silent letters were added in the 16th century to make the words reflect their Latin roots.

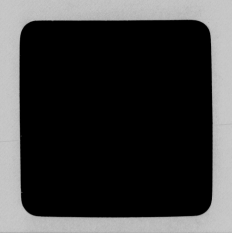

① Circle the letter you cannot hear in these words.

kneel	wrap	honest	rhyme	subtle
climb	half	gnaw	column	receipt

② Say the word on each envelope. Then write the word in the correct letterbox below.

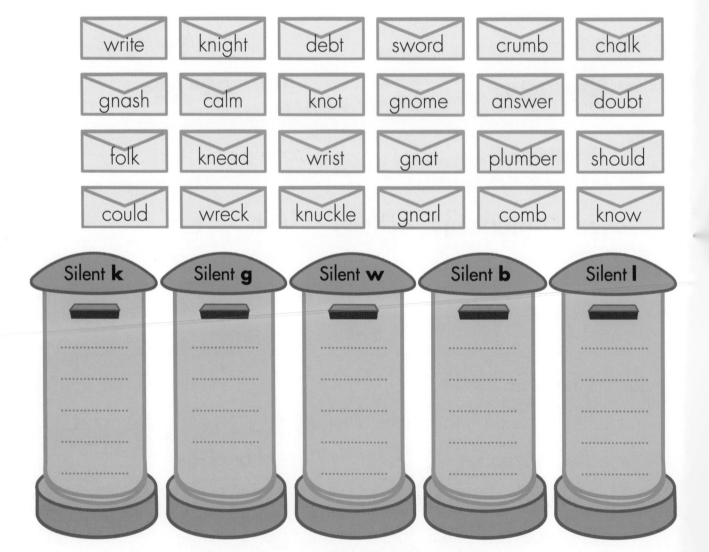

write   knight   debt   sword   crumb   chalk

gnash   calm   knot   gnome   answer   doubt

folk   knead   wrist   gnat   plumber   should

could   wreck   knuckle   gnarl   comb   know

Silent **k**   Silent **g**   Silent **w**   Silent **b**   Silent **l**

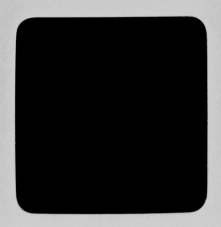

Time filler:
The letter **p** is silent when followed by either **sy** or **n** at the beginning of a word. Use a dictionary to find five words for each spelling pattern. Here are a couple of words: "psychedelic" and "pneumatic".

3 Look at question 2 on page 24 to find the answers.

Which consonants come before and after a silent **b**?

....

Which vowel sounds come before a silent **l**?

....

Which letter comes after a silent **k** and a silent **g**?

....

Which consonants come before and after a silent **w**?

....

4 Complete each of these words with its silent letter.

 ......nife

$40 + 12 = 53$ ✗ ......rong

 cu..board

 yo..k

 lam......

 ......onour

Adding -**ful** and -**ly**

Note how each suffix affects its root word. Start the timer!

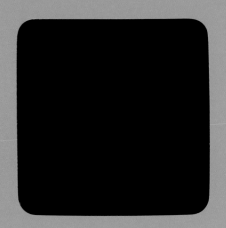

① When the word "full" becomes the suffix -**ful**, the final **l** is dropped. Write each of these as one word.

full of truth = ...   full of wonder = ...

full of cheer = ...   full of play = ...

② Add the suffix -**ful** straight on to most root words unless they end in **y**. Complete these words.

Hint: Change **y** to **i** if there is a consonant before the **y**.

beauty + full = ...   plenty + full = ...

care + full = ...   power + full = ...

③ The suffix -**ly** is added to an adjective to form an adverb.
Note: An adverb is a word that describes an action.

quick + ly = ...   slow + ly = ...

④ If the root word ends in a **y**, then change **y** to **i**. Complete these words.

speedy + ly = ...   happy + ly = ...

⑤ If the root word ends in **le**, change **le** to -**ly**. Complete these words.

gentle + ly = ...   simple + ly = ...

noble + ly = ...   humble + ly = ...

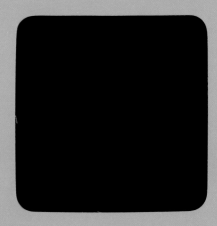

Time filler:
If you find some words tricky, make a story using its letters. To remember "accidentally" with its double **c** and an **ally**, you could make a story about two cats that accidentally scratched your ally (friend). Now you try to create a story about a special ally for "especially".

(6) If the root word ends in **ic**, then add the letters **ally**.
Change these words to adverbs.

basic ....   frantic ....   dramatic ....

(7) Drop the **e** before adding **-ly** to these words.

true + ly = ...   whole + ly = ...

(8) Complete the chart below.

Adjective	Adverb
kind	
quiet	
	strangely
famous	
	normally
general	
sudden	
	magically
hopeful	
	thankfully

Adjective	Adverb
easy	
	heavily
fateful	
noisy	
	loyally
	readily
music	
sympathetic	
	possibly
terrible	

Apostrophes

Apostrophes are used to mark the place of missing letters and to show that something belongs to someone or something.

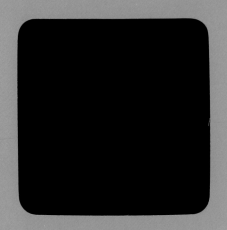

① What are the missing letters in these words?

it's ....   isn't ....   they're ....

I've ....   can't ....   we'll ....

② Make these words into one word using an apostrophe.

I am ....   he had ....   do not ....

she would ....   you will ....   does not ....

③ Join the words with their contractions.

should not	o'clock
of the clock	shouldn't
pick and mix	aren't
are not	pick 'n' mix

④ Rewrite the sentences in the speech bubbles, using contractions.

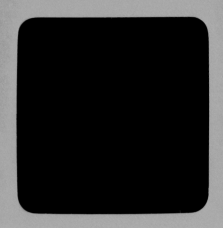

(5) An apostrophe is put after the owner's name to show something belongs to him or her. If the owner's name is a plural that does not end in **s**, then add an apostrophe and an **s**. Complete these words.

Tim.... dog.   The women.... group.

The dog.... bone.   The children.... game.

(6) If the owner's name is singular but already ends in **s**, then still add an apostrophe and an **s**.

James.... bat.   The actress.... costume.

(7) If the owner is plural and already ends in **s**, then just add an apostrophe.

The ladies.. coat.   The dogs.. collars.

Three years.. work.   The two brothers.. cars.

(8) Sometimes contractions can be confused with possessives. Underline the correct word in the brackets for each sentence.

The children visited (they're/their) grandparents.

(You're/Your) going to be late for school.

(Who's/Whose) jumper is this?

The dog ate (it's/its) dinner.

Topic prefixes

Remembering prefixes and
their meanings helps improve
both spelling and vocabulary.
Get ready to try these!

① The prefix **auto**- means "self". Join each word to its meaning.

autograph   Able to work by itself

automatic   A person's story of his/her life

autobiography   A person's signature

② The prefix **circum**- means "round". What do each of these words
go "round"?

circumference   circumnavigate

....

③ These words begin with the same prefix. The prefix means "distant".
Write the prefix.

.... phone

.... scope

④ What number do these prefixes mean?

cent- as in century   [ ]   **tri**- as in tripod   [ ]

quart- as in quarter   [ ]   **pent**- as in pentagon   [ ]

uni- as in unicycle   [ ]   **dec**- as in decade   [ ]

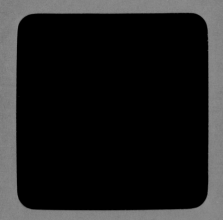

5 Here are some words with the prefix **trans**-. What does it mean?

| transmit | transfer | transport | translate | transplant |

....

6 The prefix **bi**- means "two" or "twice". Complete the crossword using **bi**- words. Use a dictionary to find the words.

Across

1. Two-footed
2. To split in two equal parts
3. Occurring every two years
4. Able to speak two languages

Down

1. Muscle with two starting points
2. Two-wheeled vehicle
3. Eyeglasses with two parts
4. Plane with two pairs of wings

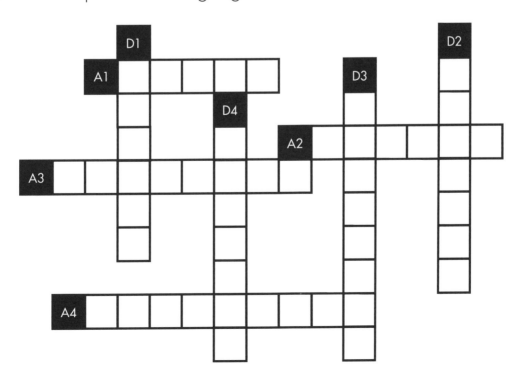

Doubling letters

Spelling a word becomes
doubly tricky when letters
are doubled. Here are a
few tips to help you.

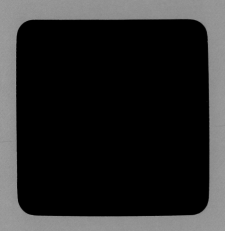

Complete these words following the doubling-letter rules.

(1) Double the last consonant when adding a suffix that begins with
a vowel to a word that ends with a vowel and a consonant.

stop + ed = ...   plan + ing = ...

fit + ed = ...   step + ed = ...

(2) Double the last consonant of a word to add a suffix when
the last syllable is stressed.

begin + er = ...   occur + ing = ...

(3) Do not double the last consonant when a word ends in
more than one consonant.

jump + ed = ...   sing + er = ...

help + ing = ...   rest + ing = ...

(4) Do not double the last consonant when the last syllable
is unstressed.

offer + ed = ...   garden + er = ...

(5) Do not double the last consonant when the suffix begins
with a consonant.

sad + ly = ...   enrol + ment = ...

6 Circle the words where the last consonant will be doubled before adding a suffix.

soak	thin	fast	pack	spot
run	walk	plan	clean	sit
comfort	disgust	drop	assist	forget
colour	grab	enjoy	reason	listen

7 In the middle of a word, letters are doubled after a short vowel sound. Complete each word and join it to its picture.

ra___it   a___le   ca___ot   che___y   pi___ow

8 In the middle of a word, letters are not doubled after a long vowel sound. Circle the words with the long vowel sound.

dinner	diner	super	supper
pole	pollen	written	writing

Crafty consonants

Some consonants are used
in specific ways in words.
Get ready to investigate
the letters **k**, **v** and **w**.

① Say these words with the "k" sound aloud. Does the sound come at the beginning, in the middle or at the end? Write the words in the chart.

| keep | rocket | token | kennel | monkey | ticket |
| king | back | tank | talk | kettle | lurk |

Beginning	Middle	End

Does a vowel or a consonant go before the **k** at the end of a word?

Write a word that rhymes with each of the words ending in the letter **k**.

....

② Say these words with the "v" sound aloud. Does the letter **v** come at the beginning, in the middle or at the end? Write them into the chart.

village   visit   five   develop   verb   river   invent   valley

Beginning	Middle	End

What do you notice about the chart? ....

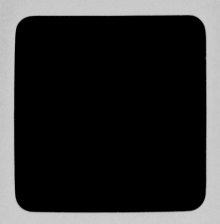

Time filler:
Try saying these tongue twisters very fast:
If two witches were watching two watches,
which witch would watch which watch?
Try this: Katy caught a kitten in the kitchen.
Which tongue twister is your favourite?

3) Underline the letter string **wa** in these words.

was   swamp   watch   dwarf   swan

wasp   swarm   toward   reward

What has happened to the letter **a**?

....

Using a dictionary, write two more words with the letter string **swa**.

....

4) Write the letter string **wo** in these words.

...... man   s......llen   ......rd

......rm   s......rd   t......

s......op   a......ke   ......nder

How many words with the letter string **swo** are in your dictionary?

....

Does the letter string **wo** mostly come at the beginning
or at the end of the word?

....

Common endings

There are three ways to
spell the "shun" sound
at the end of a word.
Give these a try!

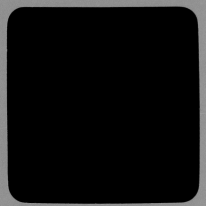

1. The most common spelling of "shun" is **-tion**. The root word usually contains a clearly pronounced vowel and is always a noun. Add **-tion** to these words.

atten............   pollu............

subtrac............

2. Use **-cian** for the names of occupations. Write these words.

electri............   musi............

politi............   magi............

3. Use **-sion** after **l**, **r** and sometimes **n**. Add **-sion** to these words.

ver............   propul............   ten............

4. Use **-sion** where the root word ends in **d**, **de**, **s** or **se** and for a soft "sh" sound. Drop the root-word endings before adding the suffix to these words.

extend + sion = ...   confuse + sion = ...

discuss + sion = ...   possess + sion = ...

5. Use **-tion**, **-cian** or **-sion** to complete these words.

posi............   pas............   physi............

educa............   opti............   mis............

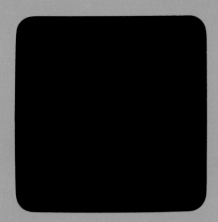

6 The **-ient** is used after **t** or **c** to make the "shunt" sound. Add **-ient** to these words.

effic..........   pat..........   anc..........

7 The **-ial** ending is used after **t** or **c** to make the "shul" sound. The **-cial** ending often comes after a vowel and the **-tial** ending after a consonant. Add **-ial** to these words.

spec......   soc......   influent......

8 The **-ure** ending is used after **t** to make the "chuh" sound or after **s** to make the "zhuh" sound. Complete these words.

moist......   meas..........   furnit......

9 The **-ous** ending makes the "us" sound and is used for adjectives. Draw a line to link each word to its meaning.

anxious   describes a meal that is tasty

ravenous   describes a person who is worried

delicious   describes an animal that is hungry

10 If there is an "i" sound before the **-ous** ending, it is usually spelt as **i**, but a few words have **e**. Circle the correct word.

serious or sereous   hidious or hideous

Homophones

Words that sound the same,
but are spelt differently and
have different meanings are called
homophones. Don't get caught out!

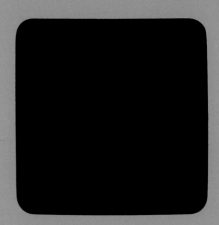

(1) Join the words that sound the same.

| peace | knot | plain | main | heard |

| mane | plane | herd | piece | not |

(2) Write a sentence for each of the words "rode", "rowed" and "road".

....

....

....

(3) Fill in the missing words to complete these sentences.

| heel | he'll | heal | too | two | to |

The runner's .... had a blister.

.... need a bandage .... let it ....

The runner had .... cuts on his leg, ...

(4) For each sentence, underline the correct word in brackets.

Turn (right/write) at the roundabout.
No one (new/knew) whose turn it was to wash up.
I can (hear/here) the birds singing.

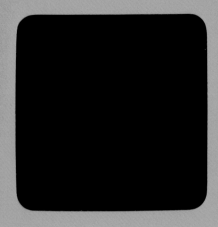

Time filler:
To distinguish between the words "stationary" and "stationery", think of an **e** in envelope and pens for "stationery" and an **a** in cars when parked are "stationary". List homophones in your spelling journal (see page 5) and make phrases to distinguish between the different words.

(5) In the table below, write these words next to their meanings.

aloud   allowed   compliment   complement

descent   dissent   precede   proceed

principal   principle   medal   meddle

Meaning	Word
Say out loud	
Permitted	
To make nice remarks	
To make something complete	
The action of going down	
A difference of opinion	
Most important person	
A truth or rule	
Go in front of	
Go onwards	
An award	
To interfere	

Tricky spellings

There are some spelling
patterns that make different
sounds in different words.
Watch out for these!

1 The spelling pattern **ou** makes different sounds.
Join the words with the same sound.

trouble   house   found

    soup

                                  loud

shout   country   coupon

cousin

    boutique   young   route

2 The spelling pattern **au** mostly makes an "or" sound.
Circle the words that make the "or" sound.

author   pause   aunt   sauce

    laugh   haunt   launch

What sound does the **au** pattern make in the words not circled?
Note: This does not occur very often.

....

3 Underline the letters that make the "ay" sound in these words.

vein   weigh   eight   convey   obey

Is the "ay" sound in the words with letters **ey**
stressed or unstressed?   ....

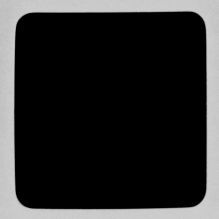

Time filler:
How many words, with three or more letters, can you make with the letters in "breakthrough"? Here are three words to get you started: "throb", "great" and "grab".

(4) The "ite" sound at the end of a word is mostly spelt with the pattern **ight**, but sometimes the letters **ite** or **yte** are used. Complete the words in these sentences with **ight**, **ite** or **yte**.

Dan dressed in a wh_____ sheet to give everyone a fr_____.

The computer had one megab_____ left.

(5) The spelling pattern **ear** makes different sounds. Join the words with the same sound.

appear   near   early

        wear

pear   ear

    rehearse   bear   Earth

(6) The letter string **ough** is tricky. Write each of the words in its rhyming group.

rough   tough   enough   cough   through   although   thought

bough   dough   plough   trough   ought   bought   though

Rhyme with puff	Rhyme with toe	Rhyme with now	Rhyme with off	Rhyme with too	Rhyme with fort

Colour the groups that only have two words or less red.

Useful word list 2

Read each column of words.
Next, cover the words up one
by one and write them. Then
move on to the next column.

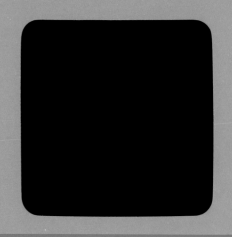

accident	earth
actually	enough
answer	exercise
arrive	grammar
bicycle	guard
breathe	heart
building	height
calendar	imagine
certain	increase
continue	interest
describe	island
difficult	knowledge
disappear	length
early	library

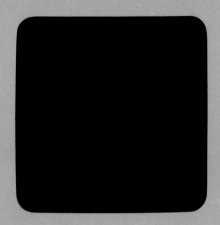

material ....

medicine ....

minute ....

occasion ....

often ....

opposite ....

particular ....

peculiar ....

position ....

possession ....

promise ....

purpose ....

quarter ....

question ....

regular ....

reign ....

remember ....

sentence ....

separate ....

special ....

straight ....

strength ....

surprise ....

though ....

thought ....

through ....

various ....

weight ....

Verb tenses

Adding -**ed** or -**ing** to the
end of a verb tells when
something happens.
Let us get started!

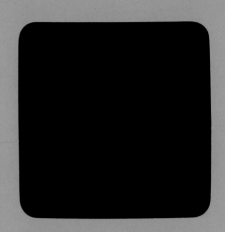

(1) Most words with short vowel sounds do not change when
adding -**ed** or -**ing**.

help + ing = ...   ask + ed = ...

(2) For a word ending in **e**, drop the letter and replace it with either -**en**
or -**ing**. Note: Some words may need to have consonants doubled.

come + ing = ...   drive + en = ...

ride + en = ...   make + ing = ...

(3) For a word that has a short vowel before its final letter and a stress
at the end, double the final letter and add either -**ed** or -**ing**.

swim + ing = ...   hop + ing = ...

refer + ed = ...   admit + ed = ...

(4) For a word ending with a vowel and a **y**, just add -**ed** or -**ing**. If a
word ends in a consonant and a **y**, change **y** to **i** before adding -**ed**.

cry + ing = ...   reply + ed = ...

play + ing = ...   enjoy + ed = ...

(5) For words ending in **c**, add a **k**, and then add either -**ed** or -**ing**.

panic + ed = ...   picnic + ing = ...

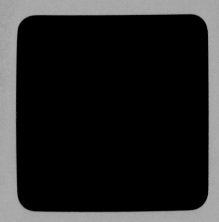

Time filler:
What happens to the words "lie" and "tie" when adding -**ing**? Which two spelling rules are used?

⑥ Add -**ing** and -**ed** or -**en** to each verb to tell what is happening now and what has happened before.

Verb	Happen**ing** now (add -**ing**)	Happen**ed** before (add -**ed** or -**en**)
look		
walk		
jump		
write		
take		
shop		
drag		
spy		
carry		
hide		

Soft sounds

In the 11th century, the French invaders of England introduced the soft "c" and soft "g" sounds into English spelling.

Sometimes the "c" sound is hard, as in **c**oat. At other times, the "c" sound is soft and has an "s" sound, as in fa**c**e.

(1) Say the words aloud and listen to the "c" sound. Is it hard or soft? Draw connecting lines.

cup

cat

mice

Hard

Soft

pencil

candle   cylinder

What letters come after the soft "c"? ....

(2) Underline the soft "c" in these words.

circle   bicycle   circuit   cyclone   accident   circus

(3) Say the words aloud and tick if the "c" sound is hard or soft.

Word	Hard	Soft
recap		
descend		
cinema		
disco		
cupboard		

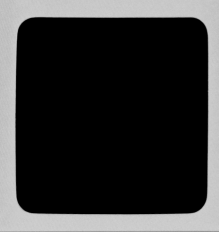

Time filler:
Learn the spelling of "special" by remembering that a CIA agent is a speCIAl agent, and to spell "fascinate" by asking, "Are you faSCInated by SCIence?"

Sometimes the "g" sound is hard, as in **g**ate. At other times, the "g" sound is soft and has a "j" sound, as in ca**g**e.

4) Say the words aloud and listen to the "g" sound. Is it hard or soft? Draw connecting lines.

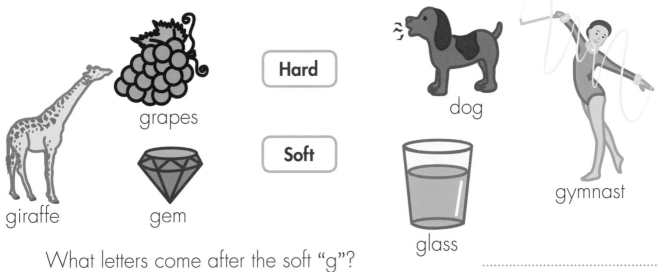

grapes

Hard

dog

Soft

giraffe   gem

gymnast

glass

What letters come after the soft "g"? ....

5) Say the words aloud and tick if the "g" sound is hard or soft.

Word	Hard	Soft
stage		
general		
garden		
Egypt		
gift		
germ		
green		

Irregular verbs

Verbs that change their vowels
when there is a change of tense
have survived from Old English.

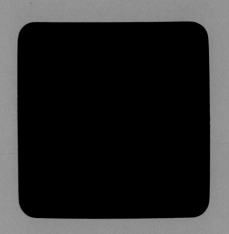

① Change these words from present tense (happening now)
to past tense (already happened). Use a dictionary if needed.
Look out for spelling patterns.

Present	Past
blow	
grow	
throw	
sing	
ring	
drink	
begin	
swim	
run	
give	
see	
hear	

Present	Past
feed	
meet	
creep	
keep	
sleep	
wear	
tear	
tell	
sell	
speak	
break	
shoot	

Present	Past
think	
fight	
buy	
take	
shake	
find	
wind	
rise	
write	
teach	
catch	
spend	

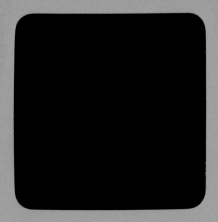

(2) Rewrite the sentences in the present tense (as if they are happening now).

I went to the beach and ate an ice cream.

....

Ken hid inside a box and made no noise.

....

Pam did her homework and then sent it to the teacher.

....

(3) Change these verbs from present tense to past participle tense
(has happened). These words usually follow "has", "have", "had"
or "was". **Note**: A participle is a form of a verb.

Present	Past participle
know	had ....
steal	had ....
fly	had ....

(4) Unscramble these letters to find four irregular verbs in the past tense.

dhel   ibtlu   meecab   rhotbug

....

More prefixes

Try adding the prefixes
on these pages and make
a note of how they affect
the meanings of the words.

(1) Add **re-** or **pre-** to these root words.

.....build ....pare .....visit .....play

.....write ....dict .....quest ....move

(2) Join the words that mean the opposite.

interior   concave

import   discord

convex   exterior

concord   export

(3) Complete this chart. For each prefix, use a dictionary to write
two more words.

Prefix	Example 1	Example 2	Example 3
a-	asleep		
be-	behind		
en-	enable		
for-	forget		
pro-	progress		

(4) Underline the prefixes in these words.

hemisphere   hyperactive   infrared

postpone   ultraviolet   underarm

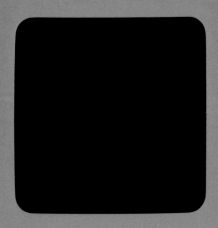

Time filler:
How many words, with three or more letters, can you make with the letters in "recommendation"? Here are three words to get you started: "mention", "comet" and "train".

(5) Write the prefixes to complete these words.

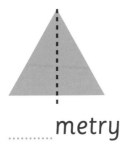

.... metry

.... circle

.... marine

(6) Find 12 words beginning with the prefixes **inter-**, **super-** and **sub-** in this word search. Write the words you find in the chart below.

s	s	u	p	e	r	n	o	v	a	i
s	u	b	m	a	r	i	n	e	s	n
u	p	s	u	b	u	n	i	t	u	t
b	e	i	n	t	e	r	n	e	t	e
s	r	s	u	b	j	e	c	t	s	r
i	v	i	n	t	e	r	a	c	t	v
d	i	n	t	e	r	v	a	l	p	i
e	s	u	p	e	r	i	o	r	e	e
d	e	s	u	p	e	r	m	a	n	w

inter-	super-	sub-

Nouns or verbs?

Adding a suffix can
change a root word into
a different part of speech.
Have a go at these!

1 Nouns and adjectives can be changed into verbs using **-ate**, **-ify**, **-en** and **-ise**. Write these words below. **Hint**: An **e** or **y** at the end of a root word has to be dropped.

elastic + ate = ...

note + ify = ...

length + en = ...

apology + ise = ...

2 Use the verb form of these words to complete the sentences.

| deep | drama | beauty |

The schoolchildren .... plays.

Models .... their faces by adding make-up.

Rivers .... when there has been heavy rain.

3 Verbs can be changed into nouns using **-tion**, **-ity** and **-ness**. Complete these words. **Hint**: Use the spelling rules for consonant and a **y** and root words ending in **e**.

reduce + tion = ...

creative + ity = ...

hard + ness = ...

happy + ness = ...

4 Change these words from verbs to either nouns or adjectives by removing or altering the suffixes.

solidify ....

quantify ....

fertilise ....

darken ....

loosen ....

activate ....

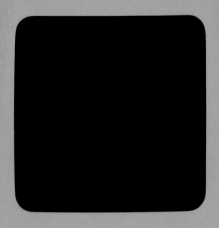

Time filler:
Finding words within words helps learn spellings. For example, visualise a rat in "sepARATe" or an ass at the end of "embarrASS". Other ways to remember spellings is working out a phrase, such as: It is only natural to go Really Red and Smile Shyly when you are embaRRaSSed.

5 Some verbs get confused with other parts of speech and are tricky and troublesome to spell. Circle the verb in each pair of words and write the meaning of the other word. Use a dictionary to help.

affect   effect   ....

accept   except   ....

advice   advise   ....

6 Nouns and verbs that are spelt the same way are called homographs. A word's meaning depends on the stress and the way it is pronounced. Find the homographs in these sentences, then circle the verbs and underline the nouns. **Hint**: Listen to how each word sounds.

The children present the thank-you present to their teacher.

The skipper had a row with the oarsmen about how to row.

The nurse wound a bandage around the wound.

I will invite you by sending you an invite.

Invitation

Adding -**able** or -**ible**

Words with similar endings can be easily muddled. There are some useful tips, but some words must be learned.

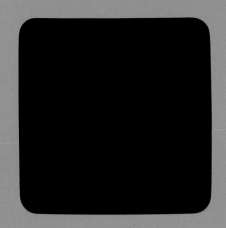

Words ending with -**able** or -**ible** are frequently confused.

(1) Often words ending in -**able** can be divided into two separate words. Write these words.

able to respect = ... able to agree = ...

able to enjoy = ... able to accept = ...

(2) Words that have **i** before the ending usually have -**able**. This ending is also often used after either a hard "c" or hard "g" sound. Add -**able** to complete these words.

reli .... soci .... amic .... navig ....

(3) When -**able** is added to words that end in **e**, remember to drop the **e**. Write these words.

breathe + able = ... value + able = ...

adore + able = ... forgive + able = ...

(4) Words ending in -**ible** cannot be divided into two separate words. Write these words.

sens + ible = ... terr + ible = ...

(5) Most words with **s** or **ss** in the middle end with -**ible**. It is also often used after a soft "c" or "g" sound. Add -**ible** to complete these words.

respons .... poss .... leg .... invinc ....

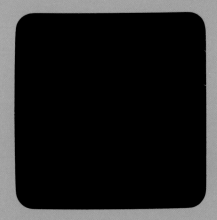

55

Time filler:
Choose five or more words
from this page and use each
one in its own sentence.
Use a dictionary to find
out the meanings.

6 Follow the -**able** and -**ible** rules to work out the endings to these words, and then find them in the word search.

break_____ imposs_____ laugh_____

ed_____ pass_____ flex_____

vis_____ revers_____ envi_____

z	i	s	m	t	e	b	i	f	r
i	m	p	o	s	s	i	b	l	e
r	e	n	v	i	a	b	l	e	v
p	a	s	s	a	b	l	e	x	e
o	s	b	i	l	e	s	s	i	r
t	v	i	s	i	b	l	e	b	s
a	o	b	l	e	i	s	a	l	i
b	r	e	a	k	a	b	l	e	b
l	a	u	g	h	a	b	l	e	l
e	l	i	d	e	d	i	b	l	e

7 For words ending in -**ative** and -**itive**, consider the corresponding word ending in -**sion** or -**tion**. If the word ends in -**ation** use -**ative**, otherwise use -**itive**. Change each of these words.

competition _____ affirmation _____

information _____ reproduction _____

ie or ei?

I before **e** except after **c**
is a well-known rhyme,
but when does it apply?

Consider the **i** before **e** rule to answer the questions below.

(1) This rule applies when the letters together make an "ee" sound.

rec__ve   th__f   rel__f

d__sel   c__ling   f__ld

p__ce   rec__pt   shr__k

(2) This rule does not apply when the letters together make
an "ay" sound.

fr__ght   __ght   n__ghbour

r__gn   v__l   w__gh

(3) This rule does not apply when using the plural form for words ending
in **cy**.

frequency   vacancy   policy

frequenc__s   vacanc__s   polic__s

(4) This rule does not apply when the letters **i** and **e** are pronounced
as separate vowels in words.

pric__r   sc__nce   soc__ty

(5) Here are some other exceptions to the **i** before **e** rule.

prot__n   s__ze   w__rd

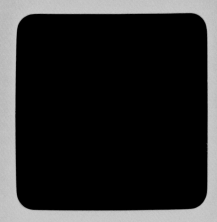

Time filler:
Remember that the word "foreign" is a foreigner that does not follow the **ie** spelling pattern, but a "fr**ie**nd" does. Make a list of words that follow the rule in your spelling journal (see page 5) and make a further column with words that are exceptions.

6 Find 10 of the words on page 56 in this word search.

r	e	d	s	e	i	e	w	c	s
e	r	e	c	i	e	v	e	i	l
c	p	i	i	c	t	h	i	e	f
e	o	s	e	i	z	e	g	l	w
i	l	e	n	w	s	c	h	i	e
v	i	l	c	f	e	i	f	c	i
e	c	f	e	i	l	d	e	n	r
p	i	w	i	e	r	i	h	g	d
r	e	t	c	l	p	e	i	t	l
s	s	i	e	d	i	e	c	s	e

Building words

Knowing root words and how to add prefixes and suffixes to them helps to spell long words correctly. Are you ready? Let us get started!

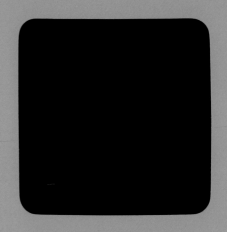

(1) Complete the chart with the long words made in each row. Keep the spelling rules in mind.

Prefix	Root	Suffix	Completed word
con-	centre	-ate	
ex-	peri	-ment	
de-	liver	-ance	
pro-	act	-ive	
bio-	graphy	-cal	
re-	verse	-ible	
ad-	vert	-ise	
pro-	duct	-ion	
inter-	nation	-al	
im-	medi	-acy	
dis-	appear	-ance	
con-	grate	-ulate	

(2) Knowing how words are related can help with spelling. Complete the root words.

Whole word	Root word
regularity	regul....
opposite	opp......
conscience	sci.........
definitely	fin....
government	gov......

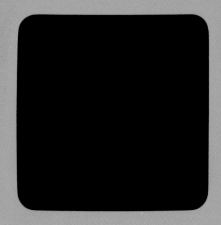

Time filler:
How many words, with three or more letters can you make with the letters in "environment"?
Here are three words to get you started: "vent", "move" and "mint".

③ Underline the root word in these words.

unbalanced   forgiveness   imprisonment

unlawful   reclaimable   forgetful

④ Underline both the prefixes and suffixes in these words.

irredeemable   adjoining   disposable

deflated   reappointment   projection

⑤ Choose a root word and a prefix and/or a suffix from the boxes to make 12 words.

Prefix	Root word	Suffix
re-	take	-ive
im-	press	-ion
dis-	cover	-ment
mis-	prove	-ing
de-	break	-able
un-	agree	

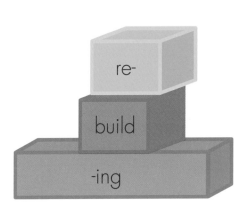

....

....

....

More suffixes

Adding or altering a suffix can make the word a different parts of speech, such as noun, adjective, verb or adverb.

Words ending in -**ant**, -**ent**, -**ance** or -**ence** have rules to help you work out what parts of speech are.

1 The suffixes determine if words are adjectives or nouns. Give these columns of words a heading either adjectives or nouns.

importance	important
distance	distant
elegance	elegant

evident	evidence
violent	violence
obedient	obedience

What endings are used for adjectives? ....

What endings are used for nouns? ....

2 Change adjectives into nouns and nouns into adjectives in the charts.

Noun	Adjective
abundance	
correspondence	
magnificence	

Noun	Adjective
	patient
	defiant
	fragrant

3 The letters **t** and **v** are often followed with -**ance**. Complete the words.

accept.......... circumst.......... relev..........

4 Verbs ending in a vowel and a **r** with a stress on the last syllable form nouns with -**ence**. Change these verbs into nouns.

differ.......... refer.......... rever..........

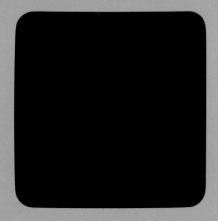

Time filler:
"Necessary" is a tricky word to spell, but you can remember it by learning the phrase: When it is neCeSSary to dreSS smartly, choose a shirt that has one Collar and two Sleeves. Add any tricky-to-spell words on this page to your spelling journal (see page 5).

(5) Some other noun endings are **-ency** or **-ancy**, meaning the state of something. Change these adjectives into nouns.

emergent ....

constant ....

vacant ....

irrelevant ....

president ....

urgent ....

Words ending in **-ary** or **-ery** also cause confusion.

(6) The ending **-ery** is less common and is usually only used in nouns. Complete these words.

batt........   myst........   machin........

gall........   cemet........   monast........   bak........

(7) The **-ary** ending is more common, so if in doubt use this ending. Complete these words.

Janu........   Febru........   diction........   secret........

libr........   contr........   necess........   annivers........

(8) Use the words in question 7 to complete these sentences.

The first month of the year is ....

A .... can help to find the meanings of words.

It was .... for the teacher to cancel the school trip.

Hyphens

A hyphen is a linking mark
between two or more words,
but do you know when you
should use it?

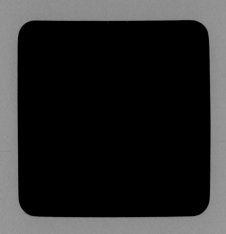

① Use a hyphen when two words are used together as an adjective
before a noun. Circle the compound adjectives.

A five-pound note   A trouble-free event

A full-length movie   A last-minute change

② Use a hyphen when joining an adjective or noun to a past-
or present-participle verb. Insert the missing hyphen.
Note: A participle is a form of a verb.

A sun dried tomato   A blue eyed doll   A hard wearing jacket

....

A well lit room   An old fashioned dress   A record breaking jump

....

③ Use a hyphen to make a group of words into an expression.
Link three words to make an expression.

do	go	one
happy	it	not
one	and	yourself
forget	to	white
black	me	lucky

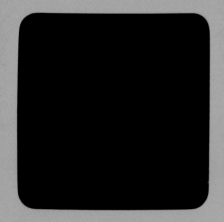

Time filler:
In your spelling journal (see page 5)
include a list of hyphenated words
that you have found in the books
you have read. This will serve as
a useful bank of words.

4) A hyphen is sometimes used to join a prefix to a word, especially
if the prefix ends with a vowel and the root word begins with one.
Correct these words.

coown ....   reenact ....   deice ....

5) A hyphen after a prefix also helps either to make the meaning of
a word clearer or to change it completely. Put a hyphen after the
prefix in each word and complete the sentence.

| relay | react | resign | recover | reform |

The artists .... their pictures.

The students .... the clay.

The builders .... the carpet.

The actors .... out the scene.

The ladies .... the chairs.

6) Some words started as two words, then were hyphenated, and are
accepted as one word these days. Use a dictionary to find out if these
words have a hyphen. Tick if correct and put a cross if incorrect.

rooftop ☐   sportswear ☐   hightech ☐

rocksolid ☐   nighttime ☐   rucksack ☐

daytime ☐   spinechiller ☐   newsflash ☐

Useful word list 3

Read each column of words.
Next, cover the words up one
by one and write them. Then
move on to the next column.

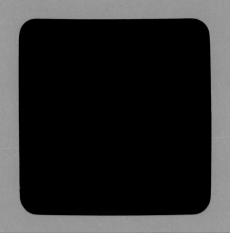

accommodate		exaggerate	
achieve		familiar	
ancient		foreign	
appreciate		frequently	
available		guarantee	
believe		identity	
committee		illustrate	
competition		immediate	
correspond		individual	
curiosity		interfere	
definite		interrupt	
dictionary		language	
embarrass		legend	
especially		leisure	

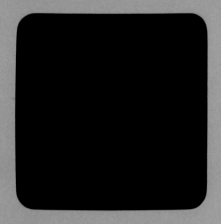

Time filler:
Choose five words from this list
and use each one in its own sentence.
Keep coming back to these lists to check
that you still know these useful words.

lightning ....

marvellous ....

mischievous ....

necessary ....

nuisance ....

occupy ....

opportunity ....

parallel ....

parliament ....

persuade ....

physical ....

programme ....

realise ....

recognise ....

recommend ....

restaurant ....

rhyme ....

rhythm ....

secretary ....

sincere ....

succeed ....

sufficient ....

suggest ....

system ....

thorough ....

variety ....

vehicle ....

yacht ....

Answers:

04–05 Syllables and stresses
06–07 Origins of prefixes

4

① Count the syllables in these words.

supermarket	4	gardening	3	furious	3
adventure	3	preparation	4	journey	2

② Link together the words that have the same number of syllables.

colour — dangerous — picture — afterwards
family — shadow — introduce — outside

③ Look at the pictures of these two-syllable words. The second syllable has been given. Have a go at spelling the first syllable.

treasure

present

④ Look at the pictures of these two-syllable words. The first syllable has been given. Have a go at spelling the second syllable.

wizard

whistle

5

⑤ A part of each label is given. Look at each picture and complete its label. How many syllables does each word have?

volcano 3   waterfall 3   mountain 2

⑥ When one syllable is longer and louder, it is a **stressed** syllable. Circle words that are stressed at the beginning, and cross out those at the end.

~~demand~~ ~~restore~~ ~~target~~ (table) (famous)

⑦ These words are spelt the same, but have different meanings when the stress changes. For each word, put a tick mark in the noun or verb column.

Word	Noun	Verb
record	✔	
re**cord**		✔
progress	✔	
pro**gress**		✔

Are the nouns stressed at the beginning or at the end? ___Beginning___

⑧ Write your name and circle the stress. How many syllables are there?

Answers will vary.

Once completed, this book aims to be a useful reference aid for remembering the rules of spellings, providing tips for tackling tricky spellings, and making links between groups of similarly spelt words. These pages provide the first tip about breaking down words into smaller more manageable chunks for each syllable. Children may clap the syllables in the words to help identify how many there are.

6

① Complete this chart of prefixes that have come from the Latin language. For each prefix, use a dictionary to write two more words, and then work out their meanings. Answers may vary.

Prefix	Example 1	Example 2	Example 3	Meaning of prefix
aqu-	aqueduct	aquatic	aquamarine	water
pro-	proceed	promote	progress	towards
im-	import	immerse	impact	into
in-, ir-, il-	incorrect	irregular	illiterate	not
pre-	preview	prepare	prevent	before
re-	redo	remake	rethink	again
sub-	submarine	subway	submerge	below
super-	superstar	superb	superhero	above
ex-	external	extinct	extract	out
co-	co-writer	co-operate	co-equal	together
de-	defrost	destruct	depart	reversal

7

② Complete this chart of prefixes that have come from the Greek language. For each prefix, use a dictionary to write two more words, and then work out their meanings. Answers may vary.

Prefix	Example 1	Example 2	Example 3	Meaning of prefix
anti-	anticlockwise	antidote	antisocial	against
auto-	autograph	automatic	autobiography	self
kilo-	kilogram	kilobyte	kilometre	thousand
cy-	cyclone	cycle	cylinder	circular
dyna-	dynasty	dynamic	dynamite	power
geo-	geography	geology	geosphere	earth
micro-	microscope	microphone	microbiology	small
mis-	misbehave	mismanage	misinterpret	hate
peri-	periscope	peripheral	perimeter	around
mono-	monorail	monosyllable	monologue	one
bio-	biology	biodiversity	biography	life

Recognising common prefixes helps children's word analysis skills and knowing the meanings supports understanding as well as decoding words. This activity encourages children to use a dictionary to find related words and look at how the prefixes have affected the meaning.

Answers:

08–09 Root words
10–11 Spellings suffixes

8

① Complete this chart of Latin and Greek root words. For each root word, use a dictionary to write two more words based on this root word, and then work out its meaning. Answers may vary.

Root word	Example 1	Example 2	Example 3	Meaning of root word
dict	dictate	dictation	dictionary	to say
pel	repel	expel	dispel	to drive
scrib	describe	prescribe	inscribe	to write
gress	progress	digress	regress	to walk
tract	attract	detract	retract	to pull
vert	divert	revert	invert	to turn
ject	eject	reject	project	to throw
dem	democracy	demonstration	democratic	people
chron	synchronise	chronology	chronicle	time
path	sympathy	pathetic	empathy	feeling
phon	telephone	microphone	symphony	sound
gram/graph	diagram	photograph	programme	write or draw
therm	hypothermia	thermal	thermometer	heat
scope	telescope	stethoscope	kaleidoscope	viewing instrument

9

② The following words are French in origin:
words with "sh" sound spelt **ch**, such as "chef";
words with "g" sound spelt **gue**, such as "tongue";
words with "k" sound spelt **que**, such as "unique".

Words with "s" sound spelt **sc**, such as "science", are Latin in origin.
Words with "k" sound spelt **ch**, such as "chorus", are Greek in origin.

Say each of the following words aloud, and then write them under the French, Italian (Latin) or Greek flags to identify the origin of the words.

school	scene	chalet	antique
chauffeur	chemist	fascinate	scissors
league	anchor	muscle	character

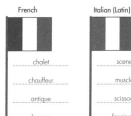

French
chalet
chauffeur
antique
league

Italian (Latin)
scene
muscle
scissors
fascinate

Greek
school
chemist
anchor
character

Encourage children to first write down words they find in a dictionary that are familiar to them and then write words that they think may be useful for them to know for their own writing. The time filler provides a strategy for learning spellings, for example, knowing that "fort" and "ate" are found in "fortunate".

10

① Complete this chart of common suffixes. For each suffix, use a dictionary to write two more words based on this suffix, and then work out their meanings. Answers may vary.

Suffix	Example 1	Example 2	Example 3	Meaning of suffix
-ship	membership	relationship	friendship	state of office
-hood	childhood	parenthood	likelihood	condition
-ness	kindness	sadness	happiness	state of
-ment	enjoyment	statement	fragment	act of
-less	helpless	useless	airless	less of
-dom	kingdom	stardom	freedom	realm
-some	wholesome	awesome	handsome	tending to be
-craft	handicraft	woodcraft	craftiness	skill in
-ology	biology	zoology	geology	study of
-ward	downward	upward	forward	in direction of
-ism	criticism	realism	activism	belief in

11

② Make words by combining each word with one of the suffixes: **-ness**, **-ment** or **-ship**. Remember: If the word ends in a consonant and a **y**, change the **y** to an **i** before adding the suffix.

silly _silliness_   agree _agreement_   drowsy _drowsiness_

merry _merriment_   partner _partnership_   close _closeness_

③ More than one suffix can sometimes be added. Write these words.

fear + some + ness = _fearsomeness_

care + less + ness = _carelessness_

④ Complete the words in the chart with the vowel suffixes **-ive**, **-ic** or **-ist**.

Suffix -ive	Suffix -ic	Suffix -ist
respons_ive_	horrif_ic_	violin_ist_
act_ive_	terrif_ic_	special_ist_
decorat_ive_	histor_ic_	art_ist_
narrat_ive_	allerg_ic_	journal_ist_

What happens to the root words ending in **e**? _The final **e** is dropped._

What happens to the root words ending in **y**? _The final **y** is dropped._

Children should be familiar with many of these suffixes, and this knowledge will help them spell words with these patterns in them. Page 11 also practises a few of the useful spelling rules regarding adding suffixes to root words ending in consonant and a **y** and root words ending in the letter **e**.

Answers:

12–13 "le" sound
14–15 Comparing adjectives

12

① The most common spelling of the "le" sound at the end of a root word is **le**. Join the rhyming words.

settle   wiggle   tumble   buckle

rumble   dimple   kettle   saddle

simple   chuckle   paddle   giggle

② Other spelling patterns that may be used for the "le" sound are **el** or **al**. In a few words, **il** or **ol** is used. Complete these words. Use a dictionary if needed.

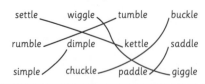

pencil   sandal   towel   aerosol

③ The "le" sound can be a suffix ending. The letters **al** are used when changing nouns to adjectives. **Note:** Sometimes the spelling of the noun must be changed slightly before adding **al**.

continent + al = _continental_   navy + al = _naval_

music + al = _musical_   nation + al = _national_

13

④ Complete the crossword. The first three letters of each word are given to you. All words have the "le" sound at the end. Use a dictionary to find the words.

Across
1. Having very hot and humid conditions (tro)
2. A celebration on the street (car)
3. A round shape (cir)
4. The remains of prehistoric living things (fos)
5. Furniture you eat at (tab)

Down
1. A human-made underground passage (tun)
2. An item or object (art)
3. A mystery or a game with interlocking pieces (puz)
4. A warm-blooded animal that has fur (mam)
5. A large building with thick walls, towers and battlements (cas)

Crossword answers:
- A1 across: tropical
- A2 across: carnival
- A3 across: circle
- A4 across: fossil
- A5 across: table
- D1 down: tunnel
- D2 down: article
- D3 down: puzzle
- D4 down: mammal
- D5 down: castle

Digraphs are a combination of two letters that make one distinct sound. The tricky part of spelling is knowing which combination to use, as often there is more than one option, like in the case of the "le" sound. Some children may recognise which spelling pattern to use by identifying the visual shape of the word. Children can make collections of the words with the different endings in their spelling journal (see page 5).

14

① Add **er** to words when you compare two things (**comparative**) and **est** when something is of the highest order (**superlative**). Complete the sentences.

Max is fast, Tom is _faster_ and Sam is the _fastest_.

Tim is tall, Dad is _taller_ and Grandad is the _tallest_.

② For words ending with an **e**, just add **r** or **st**. Complete the sentence.

The apple tree is large, the palm is _larger_, and the pine is the _largest_.

③ For words ending with a vowel and a single consonant, double the consonant and add the ending. Complete the sentence.

The Collie is big, the Greyhound is _bigger_, but the Great Dane is the _biggest_.

④ For words ending with a consonant and a **y**, change the **y** to **i** and add the ending. Use the word "angry" to complete the sentence.

John is angry, Jane is _angrier_ and Justin is the _angriest_.

15

⑤ For most three-syllable adjectives and some two-syllable adjectives, use "more" for the comparative and "most" for the superlative. Add "more" and "most" to this sentence.

The gardener is knowledgeable about plants. The tree surgeon is _more_ knowledgeable than the gardener. The botanist is the _most_ knowledgeable of all the plant lovers.

⑥ Complete the chart with the comparatives and the superlatives.

Adjective	Comparative	Superlative
slow	slower	slowest
wet	wetter	wettest
important	more important	most important
happy	happier	happiest

⑦ There are some irregular adjectives that do not follow these spelling rules. Can you link the adjective to its comparative and superlative?

Adjective	Comparative	Superlative
good	worse	best
bad	farther	least
little	better	worst
far	less	farthest

Make sure children know that adjectives are used to describe more about a noun or pronoun. These pages practise the use of adding **er** and **est** to compare two, three or more things. Often longer words sound awkward with these endings, so "more" and "most" are used in front of them.

Answers:

16–17 'Not' prefixes
18–19 Changing y

16

① The prefix **in**- is used most often. Write these words.

not direct = _indirect_

not active = _inactive_

not accurate = _inaccurate_

not capable = _incapable_

② Add **ir**- to root words beginning with **r**, making a double **r**. Write these words.

not regular = _irregular_

not responsible = _irresponsible_

not replaceable = _irreplaceable_

③ Add **il**- to root words beginning with **l**, making a double **l**. Write these words.

not legal = _illegal_

not legible = _illegible_

not logical = _illogical_

④ Add **im**- to some root words beginning with **m** and **p**. Write these words.

not mobile = _immobile_

not proper = _improper_

not possible = _impossible_

⑤ There are exceptions to the above rules. Circle the words spelt correctly.

(defrost) or infrost   irreasonable or (unreasonable)

illike or (dislike)   (depart) or inpart

(unload) or ilload   implease or (displease)

17

⑥ Add a prefix to each of these root words in the word search. Think about how the prefix changes the meaning of the root word.

credible   aware   polite   code   order
accurate   patient   made   compose   modest

i	n	c	r	e	d	i	b	l	e
m	r	i	a	i	e	u	t	n	v
p	e	m	p	r	c	n	i	i	u
a	d	p	r	o	o	m	s	m	n
t	r	o	l	m	d	a	d	m	a
i	o	l	d	t	e	d	s	o	w
e	s	i	e	o	p	e	i	d	a
n	i	t	d	s	d	i	s	d	e	r
t	d	e	c	o	m	p	o	s	e
i	n	a	c	c	u	r	a	t	e

For question 6, when deciding which prefix to use, children should first refer to the tips provided in the first four questions. If they are still undecided, they could try saying the word with each prefix and then thinking about which one sounds right. The word search will help to reinforce the pattern of the letters in the words.

18

① Add the letter **y** to these words and use the words to complete the sentences. **Hint:** For some short words, double the last consonant.

crisp	fuss	sun	run	fur	full

The bacon tasted _crispy_ .   The day was hot and _sunny_ .

The kitten was _furry_ .   The toddler was _fussy_ .

The gravy was _runny_ .   The restaurant was _fully_ booked.

② These words end with an **e**. Add the letter **y** to them. **Hint:** Drop the **e** to add the **y**.

bone	smoke	stone	grease	laze
bony	_smoky_	_stony_	_greasy_	_lazy_

Why is the **e** removed?   _When the word ends with a silent **e**,_
drop the **e** before adding the **y**.

③ Circle the words with **y** as an "igh" sound. Cross out the words with **y** as an "ee" sound.

(cry)   boy   ~~party~~   stay   ~~happy~~   (apply)

What is different about the **y** in the words not circled or crossed out?
The **y** is part of a digraph, which is a two-letter vowel blend.

19

④ Find 10 words from page 18 in this word search.

h	a	b	m	r	h	o	t	b	y
u	n	o	n	l	a	z	y	m	g
r	u	n	n	y	p	a	l	p	r
r	o	y	u	a	p	p	l	y	e
y	m	g	l	p	y	d	n	f	a
b	f	u	l	s	a	f	n	o	s
p	u	f	z	y	l	u	s	s	y
z	s	m	o	k	y	l	a	g	l
l	s	f	r	m	f	l	r	r	l
o	y	t	g	s	s	y	t	f	m

Adding **y** to make the "ee" sound at the ends of words helps to make many adjectives. Point out to children that the rules for adding the suffix **y** are similar to those for adding other suffixes, such as -**ing**. Collecting words with similar patterns in a spelling journal (see page 5) is useful to identifying and making connections.

70

Answers:

22-23 Tricky plurals
24-25 Silent letters

22

① Add **es** to each word with hissing endings: **s**, **x**, **z**, **sh**, **ch** or **ss**.

brush — brushes · glass — glasses · match — matches

② For words ending in a consonant and a **y**, change **y** to **i** and add **es**.

puppy — puppies · pony — ponies · city — cities

③ Add **s** to most words ending in an **o**.

piano — pianos · solo — solos · yo-yo — yo-yos

There are exceptions to this rule. Add **es** to make these words plural.

potato — potatoes · volcano — volcanoes · cargo — cargoes

④ For words ending in an **ff**, just add **s**.

cuff — cuffs · sniff — sniffs · puff — puffs

⑤ For words ending in an **f** or **fe**, change the **f** or **fe** to **v** and add **es**.

half — halves · leaf — leaves · knife — knives

There are exceptions to this rule. Just add **s** to make these words plural.

roof — roofs · chief — chiefs

23

⑥ Some words change completely when made plural. Match each word to its plural.

child → children
mouse → mice
goose → geese
cactus → cacti

⑦ Some other words stay the same when made plural. Circle these words below.

(deer) monkey (sheep) (fish) cat

⑧ Complete the sentences using the plural of these words.

half · fox · loaf · life · foot

Jan cut the pizza into two halves.
In the field, a fox ran to join the other foxes.
The baker cooked ten loaves of bread.
The proverb says a cat has nine lives.
The girl hopped on one foot, then she jumped on two feet.

By this stage, children will be aware that making plurals is not as simple as adding an **s** onto the ends of words. In these activities, some of the basic rules for making plural nouns are reinforced, as well as for words that are exceptions to these rules. The time filler challenges children to consider applying the rules in a creative activity.

24

① Circle the letter you cannot hear in these words.

(K)neel (W)rap (H)onest r(h)yme su(b)tle
clim(b) hal(f) (g)naw colum(n) recei(p)t

② Say the word on each envelope. Then write the word in the correct letterbox below.

write · knight · debt · sword · crumb · chalk
gnash · calm · knot · gnome · answer · doubt
folk · knead · wrist · gnat · plumber · should
could · wreck · knuckle · gnarl · comb · know

Silent **k**: knight, knead, knot, know, knuckle
Silent **g**: gnome, gnat, gnash, gnarl
Silent **w**: write, wrist, wreck, sword, answer
Silent **b**: comb, crumb, debt, plumber, doubt
Silent **l**: chalk, could, should, calm, folk

25

③ Look at question 2 on page 24 to find the answers.

Which consonants come before and after a silent **b**? — **m** and **t**

Which vowel sounds come before a silent **l**? — "a", "o" and "ou"

Which letter comes after a silent **k** and a silent **g**? — The letter **n**

Which consonants come before and after a silent **w**? — **s** and **r**

④ Complete each of these words with its silent letter.

knife · 40 + 12 = 53 ✗ wrong
cupboard · yolk
lamb · honour

These questions ask children to examine words with silent letters and to begin noticing when these may occur and which letters are likely to be silent. These words need to be learnt, but this investigation supports the memorising of these words. Encourage them to spot when silent letters appear in words, such as those mentioned in the time filler.

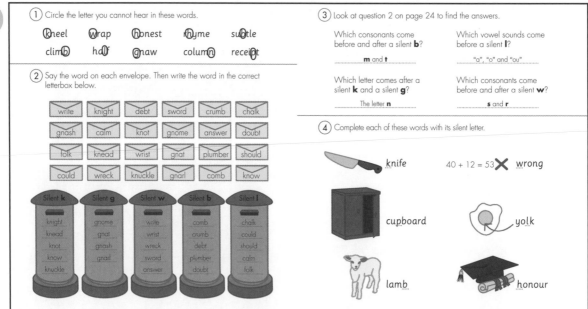

Answers:

26–27 Adding -**ful** and -**ly**
28–29 Apostrophes

26

① When the word "full" becomes the suffix -**ful**, the final **l** is dropped. Write each of these as one word.

full of truth = _truthful_   full of wonder = _wonderful_

full of cheer = _cheerful_   full of play = _playful_

② Add the suffix -**ful** straight on to most root words unless they end in **y**. Complete these words.
Hint: Change **y** to **i** if there is a consonant before the **y**.

beauty + full = _beautiful_   plenty + full = _plentiful_

care + full = _careful_   power + full = _powerful_

③ The suffix -**ly** is added to an adjective to form an adverb.
Note: An adverb is a word that describes an action.

quick + ly = _quickly_   slow + ly = _slowly_

④ If the root word ends in a **y**, then change **y** to **i**. Complete these words.

speedy + ly = _speedily_   happy + ly = _happily_

⑤ If the root word ends in **le**, change **le** to -**ly**. Complete these words.

gentle + ly = _gently_   simple + ly = _simply_

noble + ly = _nobly_   humble + ly = _humbly_

27

⑥ If the root word ends in **ic**, then add the letters **ally**. Change these words to adverbs.

basic _basically_   frantic _frantically_   dramatic _dramatically_

⑦ Drop the **e** before adding -**ly** to these words.

true + ly = _truly_   whole + ly = _wholly_

⑧ Complete the chart below.

Adjective	Adverb	Adjective	Adverb
kind	kindly	easy	easily
quiet	quietly	heavy	heavily
strange	strangely	fateful	fatefully
famous	famously	noisy	noisily
normal	normally	loyal	loyally
general	generally	ready	readily
sudden	suddenly	music	musically
magic	magically	sympathetic	sympathetically
hopeful	hopefully	possible	possibly
thankful	thankfully	terrible	terribly

These activities challenge children to use two frequently used suffixes to make adjectives and adverbs. Children may need reminding that the -**ful** suffix only has one **l**, even though it means "full of". The time filler demonstrates another way to have fun, as well as reinforcing spellings of tricky-to-spell words.

28

① What are the missing letters in these words?

it's _i_   isn't _o_   they're _a_

I've _ha_   can't _no_   we'll _wi_

② Make these words into one word using an apostrophe.

I am _I'm_   he had _he'd_   do not _don't_

she would _she'd_   you will _you'll_   does not _doesn't_

③ Join the words with their contractions.

should not ———— o'clock
of the clock ———— shouldn't
pick and mix ———— aren't
are not ———— pick 'n' mix

④ Rewrite the sentences in the speech bubbles, using contractions.
Answers may vary.

I will not be there.
It is not ready yet.
Where has everyone gone?

I won't be there.
It's not ready yet.
Where's everyone gone?

29

⑤ An apostrophe is put after the owner's name to show something belongs to him or her. If the owner's name is a plural that does not end in **s**, then add an apostrophe and an **s**. Complete these words.

Tim_'s_ dog.   The women_'s_ group.

The dog_'s_ bone.   The children_'s_ game.

⑥ If the owner's name is singular but already ends in **s**, then still add an apostrophe and an **s**.

James_'s_ bat.   The actress_'s_ costume.

⑦ If the owner is plural and already ends in **s**, then just add an apostrophe.

The ladies_'_ coat.   The dogs_'_ collars.

Three years_'_ work.   The two brothers_'_ cars.

⑧ Sometimes contractions can be confused with possessives. Underline the correct word in the brackets for each sentence.

The children visited (they're/_their_) grandparents.

(_You're_/Your) going to be late for school.

(Who's/_Whose_) jumper is this?

The dog ate (it's/_its_) dinner.

These pages tackle both examples of when to use apostrophes: for contractions and for possessive nouns. If children need further support or are not confident, explain and practise each use separately. Other answers to question 4 are "I'll not be there." and "It isn't ready yet." Questions 6 and 7 explain when to add an apostrophe when the owner's name already has an **s**.

Answers:

30–31 Topic prefixes
32–33 Doubling letters

30

1. The prefix **auto-** means "self". Join each word to its meaning.

autograph → A person's signature
automatic → Able to work by itself
autobiography → A person's story of his/her life

2. The prefix **circum-** means "round". What do each of these words go "round"?

circumference — Circle

circumnavigate — World

3. These words begin with the same prefix. The prefix means "distant". Write the prefix.

telephone

telescope

4. What number do these prefixes mean?

cent- as in century — 100
quart- as in quarter — 4
uni- as in unicycle — 1

tri- as in tripod — 3
pent- as in pentagon — 5
dec- as in decade — 10

31

5. Here are some words with the prefix **trans-**. What does it mean?

| transmit | transfer | transport | translate | transplant |

Across

6. The prefix **bi-** means "two" or "twice". Complete the crossword using **bi-** words. Use a dictionary to find the words.

Across
1. Two-footed
2. To split in two equal parts
3. Occurring every two years
4. Able to speak two languages

Down
1. Muscle with two starting points
2. Two-wheeled vehicle
3. Eyeglasses with two parts
4. Plane with two pairs of wings

Crossword answers:
- A1 Across: biped
- A2 Across: bisect
- A3 Across: biennial
- A4 Across: bilingual
- D1 Down: biceps
- D2 Down: bicycle
- D3 Down: bifocals
- D4 Down: biplane

These challenges explore further prefixes that may appear in words used in children's topic work in subjects such as maths, science and geography. Knowing what the prefixes mean as well as how to spell them will help with children's awareness of family of words with similar spelling patterns and links in meaning.

32

Complete these words following the doubling-letter rules.

1. Double the last consonant when adding a suffix that begins with a vowel to a word that ends with a vowel and a consonant.

stop + ed = stopped   plan + ing = planning
fit + ed = fitted   step + ed = stepped

2. Double the last consonant of a word to add a suffix when the last syllable is stressed.

begin + er = beginner   occur + ing = occurring

3. Do not double the last consonant when a word ends in more than one consonant.

jump + ed = jumped   sing + er = singer
help + ing = helping   rest + ing = resting

4. Do not double the last consonant when the last syllable is unstressed.

offer + ed = offered   garden + er = gardener

5. Do not double the last consonant when the suffix begins with a consonant.

sad + ly = sadly   enrol + ment = enrolment

33

6. Circle the words where the last consonant will be doubled before adding a suffix.

soak	(thin)	fast	pack	(spot)
(run)	walk	(plan)	clean	(sit)
comfort	disgust	(drop)	assist	(forget)
colour	(grab)	enjoy	reason	listen

7. In the middle of a word, letters are doubled after a short vowel sound. Complete each word and join it to its picture.

rabbit   apple   carrot   cherry   pillow

8. In the middle of a word, letters are not doubled after a long vowel sound. Circle the words with the long vowel sound.

dinner   (diner)   (super)   supper
(pole)   pollen   written   (writing)

These pages give two examples of when letters may be doubled in words; first, when adding suffixes to certain types of words, and second, after a short vowel in the middle of words. Children can refer back to this page, once completed. Encourage children to create rhymes for longer words with double letters.

Answers:

34–35 Crafty consonants
36–37 Common endings

34

① Say these words with the "k" sound aloud. Does the sound come at the beginning, in the middle or at the end? Write the words in the chart.

keep rocket token kennel monkey ticket
king back tank talk kettle lurk

Beginning	Middle	End
keep	rocket	back
king	token	tank
kettle	monkey	talk
kennel	ticket	lurk

Does a vowel or a consonant go before the **k** at the end of a word?

A consonant

Write a word that rhymes with each of the words ending in the letter **k**.

Answers may vary.

② Say these words with the "v" sound aloud. Does the letter **v** come at the beginning, in the middle or at the end? Write them into the chart.

village visit five develop verb river invent valley

Beginning	Middle	End
village	five	
visit	develop	
verb	river	
valley	invent	

What do you notice about the chart? There are no words ending in **v**.

35

③ Underline the letter string **wa** in these words.

w<u>a</u>s sw<u>a</u>mp w<u>a</u>tch dw<u>a</u>rf sw<u>a</u>n
w<u>a</u>sp sw<u>a</u>rm tow<u>a</u>rd rew<u>a</u>rd

What has happened to the letter **a**?

The letter acts like the letter **o**.

Using a dictionary, write two more words with the letter string **swa**.

Answers will vary.

④ Write the letter string **wo** in these words.

w<u>o</u>man sw<u>o</u>llen w<u>o</u>rd
w<u>o</u>rm sw<u>o</u>rd tw<u>o</u>
sw<u>oo</u>p aw<u>o</u>ke w<u>o</u>nder

How many words with the letter string **swo** are in your dictionary?

Answers will vary.

Does the letter string **wo** mostly come at the beginning or at the end of the word?

At the beginning.

Praise your child's efforts and achievements throughout this work and point out any mistakes in a positive, encouraging way. Even with an awareness of the various spelling rules, learning how to spell and choosing which letters to use is not always obvious. Children could collect tricky words or similar words in the spelling journal.

36

① The most common spelling of "shun" is **-tion**. The root word usually contains a clearly pronounced vowel and is always a noun. Add **-tion** to these words.

attention pollution
subtraction

② Use **-cian** for the names of occupations. Write these words.

electrician musician
politician magician

③ Use **-sion** after **l**, **r** and sometimes **n**. Add **-sion** to these words.

version propulsion tension

④ Use **-sion** where the root word ends in **d**, **de**, **s** or **se** and for a soft "sh" sound. Drop the root-word endings before adding the suffix to these words.

extend + sion = extension confuse + sion = confusion
discuss + sion = discussion possess + sion = possession

⑤ Use **-tion**, **-cian** or **-sion** to complete these words.

position passion physician
education optician mission

37

⑥ The **-ient** is used after **t** or **c** to make the "shunt" sound. Add **-ient** to these words.

efficient patient ancient

⑦ The **-ial** ending is used after **t** or **c** to make the "shul" sound. The **-cial** ending often comes after a vowel and the **-tial** ending after a consonant. Add **-ial** to these words.

special social influential

⑧ The **-ure** ending is used after **t** to make the "chuh" sound or after **s** to make the "zhuh" sound. Complete these words.

moisture measure furniture

⑨ The **-ous** ending makes the "us" sound and is used for adjectives. Draw a line to link each word to its meaning.

anxious — describes a meal that is tasty
ravenous — describes a person who is worried
delicious — describes an animal that is hungry

⑩ If there is an "i" sound before the **-ous** ending, it is usually spelt as **i**, but a few words have **e**. Circle the correct word.

(serious) or sereous   hidious or (hideous)

These questions refer to some of the trickier spelling pattern endings in words. There are a handful of useful tips to help remember. If children are struggling to identify the correct spelling pattern then encourage them to use strategies such as making phrases with the letters of the word or looking for words within the word.

Answers:

38–39 Homophones
40–41 Tricky spellings

38

(1) Join the words that sound the same.

peace — piece
knot — not
plain — plane
main — mane
heard — herd

(2) Write a sentence for each of the words "rode", "rowed" and "road".

.... Answers will vary. ....
.... Answers will vary. ....
.... Answers will vary. ....

(3) Fill in the missing words to complete these sentences.

| heel | he'll | heal | too | two | to |

The runner's __heel__ had a blister.
__He'll__ need a bandage __to__ let it __heal__.
The runner had __two__ cuts on his leg, __too__.

(4) For each sentence, underline the correct word in brackets.

Turn (<u>right</u>/write) at the roundabout.
No one (new/<u>knew</u>) whose turn it was to wash up.
I can (<u>hear</u>/here) the birds singing.

39

(5) In the table below, write these words next to their meanings.

aloud   allowed   compliment   complement
descent   dissent   precede   proceed
principal   principle   medal   meddle

Meaning	Word
Say out loud	aloud
Permitted	allowed
To make nice remarks	compliment
To make something complete	complement
The action of going down	descent
A difference of opinion	dissent
Most important person	principal
A truth or rule	principle
Go in front of	precede
Go onwards	proceed
An award	medal
To interfere	meddle

Activities about homophones can be fun as children get to see how words sound the same, but are spelt differently and mean something different. They also demonstrate to children how careful and aware they need to be when writing. Encourage children to use a dictionary to find the right words and check their answers.

40

(1) The spelling pattern **ou** makes different sounds. Join the words with the same sound.

trouble
soup
house
found
shout
country
loud
cousin
coupon
boutique
young
route

(2) The spelling pattern **au** mostly makes an "or" sound. Circle the words that make the "or" sound.

(author)   (pause)   aunt   (sauce)

laugh   (haunt)   (launch)

What sound does the **au** pattern make in the words not circled?
Note: This does not occur very often.

.... "ah" sound ....

(3) Underline the letters that make the "ay" sound in these words.

v<u>ei</u>n   w<u>ei</u>gh   <u>ei</u>ght   conv<u>ey</u>   ob<u>ey</u>

Is the "ay" sound in the words with letters **ey** stressed or unstressed? .... Stressed ....

41

(4) The "ite" sound at the end of a word is mostly spelt with the pattern **ight**, but sometimes the letters **ite** or **yte** are used. Complete the words in these sentences with **ight**, **ite** or **yte**.

Dan dressed in a wh<u>ite</u> sheet to give everyone a fr<u>ight</u>.

The computer had one megab<u>yte</u> left.

(5) The spelling pattern **ear** makes different sounds. Join the words with the same sound.

appear — near
wear — early
pear — ear
rehearse — bear
Earth

(6) The letter string **ough** is tricky. Write each of the words in its rhyming group.

rough   tough   enough   cough   through   although   thought
bough   dough   plough   trough   ought   bought   though

Rhyme with puff	Rhyme with toe	Rhyme with now	Rhyme with off	Rhyme with too	Rhyme with fort
rough	although	bough	cough	through	thought
tough	dough	plough	trough		ought
enough	though				bought

Colour the groups that only have two words or less red.

Encourage children to say the words aloud as they complete them, so that they connect the spelling pattern with the sound used. If children are keeping a spelling journal, encourage them to list these words as same-sounding words and then add to each list as they come across words in their reading and other language work.

Answers:

44–45 Verb tenses
46–47 Soft sounds

44

① Most words with short vowel sounds do not change when adding **-ed** or **-ing**.

help + ing = __helping__   ask + ed = __asked__

② For a word ending in **e**, drop the letter and replace it with either **-en** or **-ing**. Note: Some words may need to have consonants doubled.

come + ing = __coming__   drive + en = __driven__

ride + en = __ridden__   make + ing = __making__

③ For a word that has a short vowel before its final letter and a stress at the end, double the final letter and add either **-ed** or **-ing**.

swim + ing = __swimming__   hop + ing = __hopping__

refer + ed = __referred__   admit + ed = __admitted__

④ For a word ending with a vowel and a **y**, just add **-ed** or **-ing**. If a word ends in a consonant and a **y**, change **y** to **i** before adding **-ed**.

cry + ing = __crying__   reply + ed = __replied__

play + ing = __playing__   enjoy + ed = __enjoyed__

⑤ For words ending in **c**, add a **k**, and then add either **-ed** or **-ing**.

panic + ed = __panicked__   picnic + ing = __picnicking__

45

⑥ Add **-ing** and **-ed** or **-en** to each verb to tell what is happening now and what has happened before.

Verb	Happen**ing** now (add **-ing**)	Happen**ed** before (add **-ed** or **-en**)
look	looking	looked
walk	walking	walked
jump	jumping	jumped
write	writing	written
take	taking	taken
shop	shopping	shopped
drag	dragging	dragged
spy	spying	spied
carry	carrying	carried
hide	hiding	hidden

As children make various verbs while answering the questions, they should be aware of the **e** ending, the short vowel and consonant ending, the consonant and **y** ending, and the **c** ending. Discuss how the spelling rules are working on certain words to reinforce children's understanding so this can be applied for other words.

46

Sometimes the "c" sound is hard, as in **c**oat. At other times, the "c" sound is soft and has an "s" sound, as in fa**c**e.

① Say the words aloud and listen to the "c" sound. Is it hard or soft? Draw connecting lines.

Hard — cup, cat, cylinder
Soft — mice, candle, pencil

What letters come after the soft "c"? __Letters **e**, **i** and **y**.__

② Underline the soft "c" in these words.

c̲ircle   bic̲ycle   c̲ircuit   c̲yclone   ac̲cident   c̲ircus

③ Say the words aloud and tick if the "c" sound is hard or soft.

Word	Hard	Soft
recap	✔	
descend		✔
cinema		✔
disco	✔	
cupboard	✔	

47

Sometimes the "g" sound is hard, as in **g**ate. At other times, the "g" sound is soft and has a "j" sound, as in ca**g**e.

④ Say the words aloud and listen to the "g" sound. Is it hard or soft? Draw connecting lines.

Hard — grapes, dog, glass
Soft — giraffe, gem, gymnast

What letters come after the soft "g"? __Letters **e**, **y** and **i**.__

⑤ Say the words aloud and tick if the "g" sound is hard or soft.

Word	Hard	Soft
stage		✔
general		✔
garden	✔	
Egypt		✔
gift	✔	
germ		✔
green	✔	

Investigating the hard and soft "c" and "g" sounds will help children listen out for the soft sound and not to be caught out by the spelling. For the soft "c" sound, children are likely to use the letter **s** and for the soft "g" sound, use the letter **j**. Encourage children to look out for the letters **e**, **i** and **y** that come after the soft sounds.

Answers:

48–49 Irregular verbs
50–51 More prefixes

48

① Change these words from present tense (happening now) to past tense (already happened). Use a dictionary if needed. Look out for spelling patterns.

Present	Past
blow	blew
grow	grew
throw	threw
sing	sang
ring	rang
drink	drank
begin	began
swim	swam
run	ran
give	gave
see	saw
hear	heard

Present	Past
feed	fed
meet	met
creep	crept
keep	kept
sleep	slept
wear	wore
tear	tore
tell	told
sell	sold
speak	spoke
break	broke
shoot	shot

Present	Past
think	thought
fight	fought
buy	bought
take	took
shake	shook
find	found
wind	wound
rise	rose
write	wrote
teach	taught
catch	caught
spend	spent

49

② Rewrite the sentences in the present tense (as if they are happening now).

I went to the beach and ate an ice cream.
I go to the beach and eat an ice cream.

Ken hid inside a box and made no noise.
Ken hides inside a box and makes no noise.

Pam did her homework and then sent it to the teacher.
Pam does her homework and then sends it to the teacher.

③ Change these verbs from present tense to past participle tense (has happened). These words usually follow "has", "have", "had" or "was". **Note**: A participle is a form of a verb.

Present	Past participle
know	had _known_
steal	had _stolen_
fly	had _flown_

④ Unscramble these letters to find four irregular verbs in the past tense.

dhel	ibtlu	meecab	rhotbug
held	_built_	_became_	_brought_

Verbs that do not follow any spelling pattern rule need to be learnt. Throughout this stage, children will slowly grow aware that there are verbs that completely change when moving from tense to tense. If your child uses the verb incorrectly, repeat the sentence with the correct usage so that these irregular verbs are reinforced. Point out the use of tenses when your child is reading other materials, too.

50

① Add **re-** or **pre-** to these root words.

_re_build _pre_pare _re_visit _re_play
_re_write _pre_dict _re_quest _re_move

② Join the words that mean the opposite.

interior → exterior
import → export
convex → concave
concord → discord

③ Complete this chart. For each prefix, use a dictionary to write two more words. Answers may vary.

Prefix	Example 1	Example 2	Example 3
a-	asleep	amiss	awash
be-	behind	beneath	below
en-	enable	enact	enchant
for-	forget	forbid	forsake
pro-	progress	project	proceed

④ Underline the prefixes in these words.

_hemi_sphere _hyper_active _infra_red
_post_pone _ultra_violet _under_arm

51

⑤ Write the prefixes to complete these words.

symmetry   semicircle   submarine

⑥ Find 12 words beginning with the prefixes **inter-**, **super-** and **sub-** in this word search. Write the words you find in the chart below.

s	s	u	p	e	r	n	o	v	a	i
s	u	b	m	a	r	i	n	e	s	n
u	p	s	u	b	u	n	i	t	u	t
b	e	i	n	t	e	r	n	e	t	e
s	r	s	u	b	j	e	c	t	s	r
i	v	n	t	e	r	a	c	t	v	
d	i	n	t	e	r	v	a	l	p	i
e	s	u	p	e	r	i	o	r	e	e
d	e	s	u	p	e	r	m	a	n	w

inter-	super-	sub-
interview	supervise	submarine
interval	supernova	subject
interact	superior	subside
internet	superman	subunit

These final pages cover some more prefixes that children may use frequently, such as **re-**, **pre-**, **inter-** and **pro-**. The time filler activity can be played with any word and as a competition between members of the family to see who can find the most words, with extra points for the person with the longest word.

Answers:

52–53 Nouns or verbs?
54–55 Adding -**able** or -**ible**

52

① Nouns and adjectives can be changed into verbs using -**ate**, -**ify**, -**en** and -**ise**. Write these words below. **Hint**: An **e** or **y** at the end of a root word has to be dropped.

elastic + ate = __elasticate__   note + ify = __notify__

length + en = __lengthen__   apology + ise = __apologise__

② Use the verb form of these words to complete the sentences.

| deep   drama   beauty |

The schoolchildren __dramatise__ plays.

Models __beautify__ their faces by adding make-up.

Rivers __deepen__ when there has been heavy rain.

③ Verbs can be changed into nouns using -**tion**, -**ity** and -**ness**. Complete these words. **Hint**: Use the spelling rules for consonant and a **y** and root words ending in **e**.

reduce + tion = __reduction__   creative + ity = __creativity__

hard + ness = __hardness__   happy + ness = __happiness__

④ Change these words from verbs to either nouns or adjectives by removing or altering the suffixes.

solidify __solid__   quantify __quantity__   fertilise __fertilisation__

darken __dark__   loosen __loose__   activate __activity__

53

⑤ Some verbs get confused with other parts of speech and are tricky and troublesome to spell. Circle the verb in each pair of words and write the meaning of the other word. Use a dictionary to help.

(affect)   effect   __"Effect" means a result of an action.__

(accept)   except   __"Except" means excluding something.__

advice   (advise)   __"Advice" means a recommendation.__

⑥ Nouns and verbs that are spelt the same way are called homographs. A word's meaning depends on the stress and the way it is pronounced. Find the homographs in these sentences, then circle the verbs and underline the nouns. **Hint**: Listen to how each word sounds.

The children (present) the thank-you present to their teacher.

The skipper had a row with the oarsmen about how to (row)

The nurse (wound) a bandage around the wound.

I will (invite) you by sending you an invite.

These pages explore how nouns and verbs can be created by adding suffixes and prefixes or changing the stress on words. After children have completed these questions, ask them to think of other words they may know as examples for each one.

54

Words ending with -**able** or -**ible** are frequently confused.

① Often words ending in -**able** can be divided into two separate words. Write these words.

able to respect = __respectable__   able to agree = __agreeable__

able to enjoy = __enjoyable__   able to accept = __acceptable__

② Words that have **i** before the ending usually have -**able**. This ending is also often used after either a hard "c" or hard "g" sound. Add -**able** to complete these words.

reliable   sociable   amicable   navigable

③ When -**able** is added to words that end in **e**, remember to drop the **e**. Write these words.

breathe + able = __breathable__   value + able = __valuable__

adore + able = __adorable__   forgive + able = __forgivable__

④ Words ending in -**ible** cannot be divided into two separate words. Write these words.

sens + ible = __sensible__   terr + ible = __terrible__

⑤ Most words with **s** or **ss** in the middle end with -**ible**. It is also often used after a soft "c" or "g" sound. Add -**ible** to complete these words.

responsible   possible   legible   invincible

55

⑥ Follow the -**able** and -**ible** rules to work out the endings to these words, and then find them in the word search.

breakable	impossible	laughable
edible	passable	flexible
visible	reversible	enviable

z	i	s	m	t	e	b	i	f	r
i	m	p	o	s	s	i	b	l	e
r	e	n	v	i	a	b	l	e	v
p	a	s	s	a	b	l	e	x	e
o	s	b	i	l	e	s	s	i	r
t	v	i	s	i	b	l	e	b	s
a	o	b	l	e	i	s	a	l	i
b	r	e	a	k	a	b	l	e	b
l	a	u	g	h	a	b	l	e	l
e	l	i	d	e	d	i	b	l	e

⑦ For words ending in -**ative** and -**itive**, consider the corresponding word ending in -**sion** or -**tion**. If the word ends in -**ation** use -**ative**, otherwise use -**itive**. Change each of these words.

competition __competitive__   affirmation __affirmative__

information __informative__   reproduction __reproductive__

These exercises provide some of the tips to consider when deciding whether to use -**able** or -**ible**, and -**ative** or -**itive** at the ends of words. Crosswords and word searches are useful exercises for helping children become familiar with the patterns of letters in words. Children may wish to design their own crosswords and word searches with their tricky spellings.

Answers:

56–57 ie or ei?
58–59 Building words

56

Consider the **i** before **e** rule to answer the questions below.

1. This rule applies when the letters together make an "ee" sound.

rec<u>ei</u>ve	th<u>ie</u>f	rel<u>ie</u>f
d<u>ie</u>sel	c<u>ei</u>ling	f<u>ie</u>ld
p<u>ie</u>ce	rec<u>ei</u>pt	shr<u>ie</u>k

2. This rule does not apply when the letters together make an "ay" sound.

fr<u>ei</u>ght	<u>ei</u>ght	n<u>ei</u>ghbour
r<u>ei</u>gn	v<u>ei</u>l	w<u>ei</u>gh

3. This rule does not apply when using the plural form for words ending in **cy**.

frequency	vacancy	policy
frequenc<u>ie</u>s	vacanc<u>ie</u>s	polic<u>ie</u>s

4. This rule does not apply when the letters **i** and **e** are pronounced as separate vowels in words.

pric<u>ie</u>r	sc<u>ie</u>nce	soc<u>ie</u>ty

5. Here are some other exceptions to the **i** before **e** rule.

prot<u>ei</u>n	s<u>ei</u>ze	w<u>ei</u>rd

57

6. Find 10 of the words on page 56 in this word search.

r	e	d	s	e	i	e	w	c	s
e	r	e	c	i	e	y	e	i	l
c	p	i	i	c	t	h	i	e	f
e	o	s	e	i	z	e	g	l	w
i	l	e	n	w	s	c	h	i	e
v	i	l	c	f	e	i	f	c	i
e	c	f	e	i	l	d	e	n	r
p	i	w	i	e	r	i	h	g	d
r	e	t	c	l	p	e	i	t	l
s	s	i	e	d	i	e	c	s	e

This commonly known "**i** before **e**" rhyme is helpful only up to a point, as it is only applicable to words containing the "ee" sound. The questions on page 56 help children learn about the many exceptions to this rule, including plurals and when vowels are pronounced separately in words.

58

1. Complete the chart with the long words made in each row. Keep the spelling rules in mind.

Prefix	Root	Suffix	Completed word
con-	centre	-ate	concentrate
ex-	peri	-ment	experiment
de-	liver	-ance	deliverance
pro-	act	-ive	proactive
bio-	graphy	-cal	biographical
re-	verse	-ible	reversible
ad-	vert	-ise	advertise
pro-	duct	-ion	production
inter-	nation	-al	international
im-	medi	-acy	immediacy
dis-	appear	-ance	disappearance
con-	grate	-ulate	congratulate

2. Knowing how words are related can help with spelling. Complete the root words.

Whole word	Root word
regularity	regul<u>ar</u>
opposite	opp<u>ose</u>
conscience	sc<u>ience</u>
definitely	fin<u>ite</u>
government	gov<u>ern</u>

59

3. Underline the root word in these words.

un<u>balanced</u>	for<u>give</u>ness	im<u>prison</u>ment
un<u>lawful</u>	re<u>claim</u>able	for<u>get</u>ful

4. Underline both the prefixes and suffixes in these words.

<u>ir</u>redeem<u>able</u>	<u>ad</u>join<u>ing</u>	<u>dis</u>pos<u>able</u>
<u>de</u>flat<u>ed</u>	<u>re</u>appoint<u>ment</u>	<u>pro</u>ject<u>ion</u>

5. Choose a root word and a prefix and/or a suffix from the boxes to make 12 words. Answers may vary.

Prefix	Root word	Suffix
re-	take	-ive
im-	press	-ion
dis-	cover	-ment
mis-	prove	-ing
de-	break	-able
un-	agree	

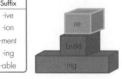

improve	depress	breakable	discovering
recovering	depressive	retake	impression
mistake	agreement	discover	disagree

These challenges show how words can be built up in parts. Continue to encourage children to reverse this process when spelling longer words, by splitting the words into smaller chunks to make them more manageable. These can be split by syllable chunks as well as by prefix, root word and suffix as practised on these pages.

Answers:

60–61 More suffixes
62–63 Hyphens

60

Words ending in **-ant**, **-ent**, **-ance** or **-ence** have rules to help you work out what parts of speech are.

(1) The suffixes determine if words are adjectives or nouns. Give these columns of words a heading either adjectives or nouns.

Noun	Adjective
importance	important
distance	distant
elegance	elegant

Adjective	Noun
evident	evidence
violent	violence
obedient	obedience

What endings are used for adjectives? **-ant** and **-ent**
What endings are used for nouns? **-ance** and **-ence**

(2) Change adjectives into nouns and nouns into adjectives in the charts.

Noun	Adjective
abundance	abundant
correspondence	correspondent
magnificence	magnificent

Noun	Adjective
patience	patient
defiance	defiant
fragrance	fragrant

(3) The letters **t** and **v** are often followed with **-ance**. Complete the words.

accept**ance**   circumst**ance**   relev**ance**

(4) Verbs ending in a vowel and a **r** with a stress on the last syllable form nouns with **-ence**. Change these verbs into nouns.

differ**ence**   refer**ence**   rever**ence**

61

(5) Some other noun endings are **-ency** or **-ancy**, meaning the state of something. Change these adjectives into nouns.

emergent _____emergency_____	irrelevant _____irrelevancy_____
constant _____constancy_____	president _____presidency_____
vacant _____vacancy_____	urgent _____urgency_____

Words ending in **-ary** or **-ery** also cause confusion.

(6) The ending **-ery** is less common and is usually only used in nouns. Complete these words.

battery   mystery   machin**ery**
gallery   cemetery   monastery   bak**ery**

(7) The **-ary** ending is more common, so if in doubt use this ending. Complete these words.

January   February   diction**ary**   secret**ary**
libr**ary**   contr**ary**   necess**ary**   annivers**ary**

(8) Use the words in question 7 to complete these sentences.

The first month of the year is _____January_____ .

A _____dictionary_____ can help to find the meanings of words.

It was _____necessary_____ for the teacher to cancel the school trip.

Children practise making links by identifying how spellings of words relate to each other in their various forms. For example, if children know how to spell "important", then they can make the connection of using the "**-ance**" spelling pattern for the noun.

62

(1) Use a hyphen when two words are used together as an adjective before a noun. Circle the compound adjectives.

A (five-pound) note   A (trouble-free) event

A (full-length) movie   A (last-minute) change

(2) Use a hyphen when joining an adjective or noun to a past- or present-participle verb. Insert the missing hyphen.
Note: A participle is a form of a verb.

A sun dried tomato	A blue eyed doll	A hard wearing jacket
A sun-dried tomato	A blue-eyed doll	A hard-wearing jacket

A well lit room	An old fashioned dress	A record breaking jump
A well-lit room	An old-fashioned dress	A record-breaking jump

(3) Use a hyphen to make a group of words into an expression. Link three words to make an expression.

do — and — one
happy — it — not
one — go — yourself
forget — to — white
black — me — lucky

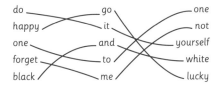

63

(4) A hyphen is sometimes used to join a prefix to a word, especially if the prefix ends with a vowel and the root word begins with one. Correct these words.

coown _____co-own_____   reenact _____re-enact_____   deice _____de-ice_____

(5) A hyphen after a prefix also helps either to make the meaning of a word clearer or to change it completely. Put a hyphen after the prefix in each word and complete the sentence.

relay	react	resign	recover	reform

The artists _____re-sign_____ their pictures.
The students _____re-formed_____ the clay.
The builders _____re-lay_____ the carpet.
The actors _____re-acted_____ out the scene.
The ladies _____re-cover_____ the chairs.

(6) Some words started as two words, then were hyphenated, and are accepted as one word these days. Use a dictionary to find out if these words have a hyphen. Tick if correct and put a cross if incorrect.
Answers may vary.

rooftop	✔	sportswear	✔	hightech	✗
rocksolid	✗	nighttime	✗	rucksack	✔
daytime	✔	spinechiller	✗	newsflash	✔

Children should be aware of how the use of a hyphen can affect the meaning of a word or a phrase. These exercises practise when hyphens are used. A hyphen should not be confused with a dash, which is longer and used to replace punctuation. The answers to question 6 may vary depending on the dictionary children are using.

Answers:

Useful words to learn to spell

The method of learning spellings using look, say, cover, write and then check is a familiar practice for many children. Encourage children to relook at these lists of words from pages 20–21, 42–43 and 64–65 on a frequent basis and test them until they are confident when spelling them accurately in their writing. Each time, praise progress and improvement. For any spellings that are causing difficulty, suggest creating phrases or finding words within words as practised in some of the time fillers. Add them to their spelling journal as a reference as well.

Monday	winter	fifteen	bicycle	island	separate	familiar	parliament
Tuesday	spring	sixteen	breathe	knowledge	special	foreign	persuade
Wednesday	summer	seventeen	building	length	straight	frequently	physical
Thursday	autumn	eighteen	calendar	library	though	guarantee	programme
Friday	January	nineteen	certain	material	thought	identity	realise
Saturday	February	twenty	continue	medicine	weight	immediate	recognise
Sunday	March	thirty	describe	minute	accommodate	individual	recommend
holiday	April	forty	difficult	occasion	achieve	interfere	restaurant
yesterday	May	fifty	disappear	often	ancient	interrupt	rhyme
tomorrow	June	sixty	early	opposite	appreciate	language	rhythm
birthday	July	seventy	earth	particular	believe	legend	secretary
anniversary	August	eighty	enough	peculiar	committee	leisure	sincere
weekend	September	ninety	exercise	position	competition	lightning	succeed
fortnight	October	hundred	grammar	possession	correspond	marvellous	sufficient
tonight	November	thousand	guard	promise	curiosity	mischievous	suggest
today	December	million	heart	purpose	definite	necessary	system
month	eleven	accident	height	quarter	dictionary	nuisance	thorough
morning	twelve	actually	imagine	question	embarrass	occupy	variety
afternoon	thirteen	answer	increase	regular	especially	opportunity	vehicle
season	fourteen	arrive	interest	remember	exaggerate	parallel	yacht